The Bastion
of
Liberty

Willem Otterspeer

The Bastion of Liberty

LEIDEN UNIVERSITY TODAY AND YESTERDAY

LEIDEN UNIVERSITY PRESS

Translated from the Dutch by Beverly Jackson

Cover design and lay-out: Suzan Beijer, Weesp
Cover illustration: P.W.M. Trap, The Rapenburg canal with the main university
building, c. 1850. Leiden Regional Archives
Illustration page 2: The Rapenburg canal in low-lying mist with the National Museum
of Antiquities in the background

ISBN 978 90 8728 030 7
NUR 680

© W. Otterspeer / Leiden University Press, 2008

Contents

Preface

The inspiration for this book was another book. My overriding concern as I was preparing the fourth volume of my history of Leiden University was that it must be different from the previous three. Modernity and scale expansion made Leiden University a different institution in the twentieth century, one scarcely comparable to what had gone before. This discrepancy prompted me to take a step back, to look briefly at where I had come from, to see where I should be going. *Reculer pour mieux sauter*, that was the rationale underlying this book.

When I submitted the proposal to my university's executive board, the response was 'Well make a readable book out of it then, a story that will be interesting to our foreign students as well as Dutch alumni'. And so it became a small, readable book, in English as well as Dutch. That is how it happened.

◄ *Weeping cherub on the funeral monument of theology professor Johannes Cocceius (1603-1669)*

Introduction

Writers seeking to express the essence of a university have used a variety of metaphors, ranging from 'citadel of conservatism' to 'vehicle of change', from 'stronghold of the ruling class' to 'house of pure learning'. Such metaphors are frequently misleading; the university is a complex institution with a long history. But the phrase 'bastion of liberty' chosen by Walter Rüegg, as editor-in-chief of the four-volume *History of the University in Europe*, is more thought-provoking. That is because besides basing himself on factual material, Rüegg also draws inspiration from hope. In his view, the alpha and omega of the university are reform and improvement. In introducing the first volume of this ambitious work, he writes that the university was conceived as the embodiment of a specifically academic ethics, which sought to improve society through a cumulative process of knowledge acquisition.

While adopting this view as the framework for the present book, I have at the same time suggested a more conservative alternative. Basing myself on the general idea of a 'bastion of liberty' as elaborated by Rüegg et al., I propose that concepts such as 'equilibrium' and 'mediation' are key to understanding the university as an institution. Taking the history of Leiden University as my example, I set out to show that a university is a form of social capital, one of Western society's answers to the dilemma of collective action, an instrument for preserving and restoring equilibrium, and hence for fostering continuity. From this vantage point, a university is a confidence-building mechanism

◄ *Neogothic bracket in the professors' gown room in the main university building*

that generates solutions to the serious problems facing society.

The scholastic humanism that spawned the university as an institution viewed each human being as a microcosm, a miniature version of the world. Human beings' complexity gave them the potential capacity to fathom the world and to strike a balance between opposing elements. As Dante writes, at the end of his *Monarchia*: 'Man is poised midway between the ephemeral and the immortal. Just as every centre has two ends, so too do human beings have a dual nature. And since every nature is predestined to serve a certain purpose, it follows that Man has two purposes: on the one hand, to seek happiness in this world, and on the other, to seek the bliss of eternal life.'

The mediaeval university too occupied an intermediate position, in this case between the two universal powers of its day. As Herbert Grundmann has shown, in a brilliant essay, the thirteenth century added a third principle to the standard doctrine of the two secular powers, *Sacerdotium* and *Regnum*, religious and political power – *Studium*, knowledge; that is, the university as *tertium comparationis* in the changing political conditions of the Middle Ages. Since it was then accepted wisdom that the power in the world was shared by three major nations, the Italians, the Germans and the French, this theory made it possible to recognise the increasing political influence of France. Thus, the University of Paris was assigned an honourable position between pope and emperor.

As 'the third way', the mediaeval university had to exert a stabilising influence, a function that was recognised by pope and emperor alike. Courses in ecclesiastical doctrine and canon law were obviously intended to bolster the central power of the pope, just as the study of Roman law and political theory was intended to bolster the claims of the emperor. But from the moment that the pope started promoting a doctrine of the faith that was based on rational foundations as a touchstone of heretical beliefs, he imposed constraints on his own freedom. And when Frederick II affirmed that the imperial throne derived its power from laws as well as the use of arms, he was effectively limiting his own scope for action.

If we then proceed to enquire how the university was embedded in mediaeval society, and seek to define the role of graduates and their careers, we

▶ *Window in the former National Herbarium, Nonnensteeg*

▲ *Ornamental work embellishing the former Chemical and Pharmaceutical Laboratory*
   on Hugo de Grootstraat

essentially find the same thing. In a world marked by enormous social diversity, and in which political and legal stability were in short supply, universities exerted a largely stabilising influence. The changes they brought about helped local or higher-ranking authorities to adjust and survive.

The mediaeval curriculum, too, structured as it was around the standard works of Aristotle, was essentially a golden mean. It sought to combine diverse types of knowledge and disciplines under a common denominator. Aristotle described scholarship as an eclectic activity, in which one tried 'as much as possible to retain the truth of all sound opinions on a particular matter, or in any case most, and the most authoritative, among them'. One should look for evidence that was *sufficient*, not necessarily *conclusive*. This was the methodological complement to Aristotle's famous 'doctrine of the mean', in which each virtue is seen as the mean between two vices and the best law is one that is feasible, rooted in a mix of democracy and oligarchy, supported by a middle class (*hoi mesoi*, literally, 'the people in the middle').

Medical and legal theory were both based on the same criterion, which lent a fundamental consistency to the mediaeval curriculum. Aristotelian philosophy contained many Hippocratic elements, and to Hippocrates, the primary authority on medical matters, common sense and equilibrium were key concepts. Health was seen as a kind of equilibrium between the different bodily fluids or humours, and different ways of life. Hippocrates' writings also had a marked impact on legal ideas, in which natural equilibrium took the form of *aequitas*: the idea that honesty and impartiality were essential to legal rules.

The same applied to theology. There is an uninterrupted tradition – from Augustine through Thomas Aquinas to Melanchthon – that saw Roman law as part of natural law, and nature as attuned to eternal salvation. The great twelfth-century ecclesiastical jurist Gratianus used dialectics to reconcile the contradictions in the writings of the Church Fathers. The rationalisation of the theological thinking of his day meant that scholars were willing to discuss every existing problem of dogma, but without any need to offer permanent solutions.

The scholastic theory of education that converted these disciplines into a curriculum was remarkably uniform in its methods. From the liberal arts to theology, these methods were based on elementary manuals, ranging from *tabula* that compressed eight books of Aristotle's *Physics* into six pages to compendiums with summaries of specific parts of the Aristotelian corpus. In fact, there is a great deal of similarity between the use of the Hippocratic aphorisms – a collection of sayings with almost allegorical expressiveness – and the two titles of the *Digest* 50.16, 'On the meaning of words' ('*De verborum significatione*') and 50.17, 'On the diverse rules of ancient law' ('*De diversis regulis iuris antiqui*'), which together constituted a fairly natural introduction to legal thinking, in much the same way that the Ten Commandments constituted a concise introduction to dogma.

The university was thus part of a glorious mediaeval cohesive whole: the religious unity of pope and Church and the political unity of emperor and state were reflected, as it were, in the scholarly unity of philosophy and biblical knowledge. The early modern period put an end to this cohesiveness. It put an end to the unity of the Church, culminating in a cacophony of competing beliefs. It put an end to the political unity of Europe and replaced it with rivalry between national states and political systems. And it also put an end to the unity of scholarship, which became fragmented into a range of rival methods.

It was humanism that evidently provided the most satisfactory answer to this fragmentation. As humanism successfully infiltrated into existing universities and the humanist inspiration for the founding of new ones, most notably in Northern Europe from the fifteenth century onwards, educational ideas of a different kind started to assert themselves. A shift of emphasis from content to method, from truth to probability, from specific to general knowledge, all influenced the curriculum and the goals of university education.

While new subjects like Hebrew and Greek appeared on the curriculum, there was also a revival of interest in old subjects such as rhetoric and ethics. Inspired by the *bonae litterae*, the curriculum attached great value to literary and historical sensitivity, which also permeated the 'higher' faculties of theology, law and medicine. Rote learning and constant repetition were the foundations of this method, and practical usefulness the main criterion of its success. Its purpose was to prepare students for public life – 'in the market and the Senate, in the people's assembly, in every kind of gathering' (*'in forum, in Senatum, in concionem populi, in omnem hominum conventum'*), as Ramus wrote – and to inculcate practical wisdom or Christian ethics.

Despite all the changes in curriculum content and the approach to studying, the objective was still the same. The humanist university still played the role of mediator – even more so, perhaps, than its mediaeval counterpart. By helping to defuse religious controversies, by supporting the state bureaucracy, and by creating ritualised forms of scholarly debate, the university had a stabilising effect on society at large. Since it provided instruction in a range of disciplines, combining study and training, it had a major impact on the structure of society, amalgamating nobility and the upper echelons of the bourgeoisie into a new élite. Leiden University, which, as one of the earliest proposals for its curriculum put it, sought to be a *'seminarium ecclesiae et reipublicae'* a school for Church and society, is one of the best examples of this mediating role.

JUSTUS LIPSIUS.

JOSEPHUS. SCALIGER. IUL. CAES. A BURDEN. FIL

ACADEMIAE LUGD.-BAT. DECUS INDE A.
D. 28 AUGUSTI. A. 1593. NATUS AQUINNI
NITIOBRIGUM. NONIS AUGUSTI. A. 1540.
OBIIT D. 21 IANUAR. A. 1609.

CAROLVS   CLVSIVS.

CAR: CLVSI ATREB: AN: LIX: EFFIGIES EXPRESSA VIEN: AVSTR: MD XXCV.

CLAUDIVS.
ÆTATIS. 40
Anno. 1636

SALMASIVS

CLAUDiUS SALMASIUS.

1

Weapons and Words

LEIDEN
UNIVERSITY

1575-1775

Contradictory Forces

The miracle that was Leiden University, an institution spun from thin air, an act of faith, arose against the backdrop of an even greater miracle, one that held Europe spellbound. Diplomats and scholars, merchants and tourists, everyone who visited the Republic of the United Provinces, rubbed their eyes in disbelief. The Republic's perfect location, its dozens of cleanly swept towns, the idiosyncrasies of its political system, the self-discipline of its people, with their technical and economic resourcefulness, their wealth and security, and above all the liberty in which they lived their lives, there seemed no end to the surprises the country had to offer.

It must be added that these same qualities roused others to the very opposite of admiration. The poverty of the soil and the unremitting compartmentalisation of the land, the impenetrability of the country's politics and the ruthlessness of its trade, the rapacity of the elite and the vulgarity of the rest, the utter lack of decorum and hierarchy, all of this was the other side of the so lavishly praised coin. One man's freedom was another man's excess. The most benevolent of observers had to concede that the United Provinces was somewhat more delightful to visit than to stay.

The United Provinces, and Holland most of all, the setting in which Leiden University plied its learning, was an amalgam of contradictory forces, oppositions that had governed the dynamics of its history. Foremost among them were those between land and water, nobles and burghers, trade and industry, monarchic and democratic inclinations, and maritime politics geared towards preserving peace versus a politics of territorial expansion. These contrasts, combined as they were with great individual freedom of conscience, generated a specific 'debating culture' in the Netherlands. Within that culture, the university occupied a prominent position. The United Provinces sought in many ways to neutralise the contradictions that shaped its distinctive identity, and the world of higher education, Leiden University, was one of the most important vehicles for doing so.

Foundation

On Tuesday, 8 February 1575, at 7 o'clock in the morning, a great crowd filled Leiden's largest church, the building once known as St Peter's. Everyone who had heeded the posters and proclamations – notices spread as far as Delft, Gouda and Rotterdam – congregated in that cold, bare church to hear its minister, Pieter Cornelisz, commend the new university of Leiden to God's grace. It would extol His name and edify His congregation, serving the industry and prosperity of town and country alike. Fostering 'salvation' and 'proficiency in all the honest and praiseworthy Arts', that was what the university was all about, this hard-headed Calvinist told his listeners. And 'learning' too, he added, although this point got a little lost between spiritual salvation and practical benefits.

This was the picture that the new Calvinist Church had of Holland's new university. The day's first academic address was also held by a minister of the church. Caspar Coolhaas, a local preacher and the first professor of theology, spoke, according to the contemporary city chronicler J.J. Orlers, 'in praise of Theology'. But other parties were also involved in the founding of Leiden University, and they too presented their vision that day.

Their vehicle was a solemn procession that departed from the town hall at 9 a.m. After a brief walk past a few very simple 'triumphal arches', they converged on the university's first premises, the former convent of St Barbara.

Companies of the civic militia marched at the front and rear of the procession. The presence of the guardsmen was only logical, explained Orlers, 'since they believed that they had secured their [city's] freedom and that it was their duty to uphold it'.

Leiden University, founded during a crucial stage of Holland's revolt against Spanish domination, embodied the two canonical reasons for that revolt: two forms of liberty, religious and political, that are very difficult to reconcile. When William of Orange, the leader of the revolt, suggested to the States of Holland and Zeeland that they found a university, he hoped to achieve 'the firm support and sustenance of freedom and good lawful government of the land not only in matters of religion, but also in matters impinging on the public good'.

He praised Leiden's suitability for the new institution. The city's prominent role in the revolt – Leiden was the second major city in Holland to have repulsed a Spanish siege – was probably the factor that swung the States in its favour. The presence in the procession of three burgomasters, the sheriff and magistrates emphasised the special ties between city and university.

The attitude of the university itself to its role in serving the church and state can be inferred from the allegorical images of the four faculties in the procession. The *pièce de resistance* of the procession was a very soberly adorned cart with *Sacra Scriptura*, the holy scriptures. Its prominent position emphasised the position of theology as the most important faculty. Then came *Justitia*, blindfold with her scales and sword, followed by *Medicina*, with herbs and a urinal. *Minerva*, armed with her shield and spear, symbolising the faculty of *artes* or liberal arts, sometimes referred to as philosophy, brought up the rear. This order reflected the customary Parisian hierarchy of subjects, which in turn reflected their importance in society.

The university's specific function as an institution serving the interests of church and city, and most notably the role it was expected to play in the new political situation, became clear as soon as the procession reached the university building. From the second bridge over Rapenburg, halfway down the canal, the procession was escorted by a small boat carrying Apollo and the nine Muses. These apparitions disembarked in front of the university and wel-

Procession marking the inauguration of the university on 8 February 1575

de Hoochwoert

S. MATHÆUS   S. SCRIPTURA

S. MARCUS

IUSTITIA

TRIBONIANUS

ULPINIANUS

S. IULIANUS   PAPINIANUS

Booden   C. Coolhasius   D. Theodo.' Nieuburgius   Fustus Menijn   P. Forestus   Laurentius ab Arschot

Jacob. vä der Does   G. Wijngaerden   De H. van Noortwijk   Artus van Brederode   F. Arent vä Diuoirde   F. vä Broeckhou   D. vä Montfoort   Willë vä Hemskerk   Willë verloo   C. van Barevelt

S. van Veen   C. Aelbrecht van Raephorst   Pieter oom Pietersoö   P. Pieter   Joris soort   Cornelis H. vä Torenvliet   D. Gerardus Bontius   Pieter H. vä Wassenaer

M. Cornelius d' groe

D. Gentius

Arcus triuphalis
voor de Universeteijt

comed the procession with some verses in Latin, written by Janus Dousa, the university's first governor.

In his poetry, Dousa deferred dutifully to the various authorities, repudiating Catholicism and the Spanish overlords in favour of a Protestant Leiden and the House of Orange. But the main theme of his verses was the role of the liberal arts in promoting peace. Neptune, who moored his boat opposite the university's new premises, said to the Muses: 'Now Muses be of good cheer, Mars himself must yield his place. For with you he can no common cause embrace.'

In Dousa's view, the university was first and foremost about wisdom and

▲   *The monastery of St Barbara on Rapenburg canal, which housed the university until 1577*

learning. The city had seen quite enough fighting already, he had Apollo tell the Muses. What it needed now was an opportunity to teach the liberal arts. And the Muses answered: 'Apollo, you will always find us at your service. Let the art of learning be our matrimonial bond.' This marriage, the unity of science and art, of learning and wisdom, would create equilibrium in the state and civilise its people. Leiden University must open its doors to the Muses, it should be a *Musarum domicilium*.

Even so, there is a certain paradox in these lines. True, they open with the rhetorical question, 'Can the Muses and Mars, art and science and the "demon of war", coexist?' 'Impossible' was the answer. 'But now, Muses, has the god of war retreated before you.' Yet the final lines, in which Justitia addresses the celebrated Roman physician Cornelius Celsus, who also wrote books about rhetoric and the art of warfare, read: 'It was your achievement to civilise what had been coarse, and no less was the splendour that your books instilled into medical science. As an orator you also discussed the virtues of the art of war, uniting Mars with the Muses.'

Weapons and Words

An anecdote is told of one Jacob Maestertius, who is described as having been born in Denmark, which he left to go to Leiden. There he arrived in tattered clothes and without a penny to his name, but in the possession of a sword and a law book. 'With one or the other,' he is as quoted as saying, 'I shall earn my living.' The chronicler who wrote all this down is rather unreliable, and the anecdote itself is full of errors – for instance, Maestertius was born not in Denmark but in Dendermonde, a little village in Flanders. But mistakes are irrelevant in this case. The story about the two ways of providing for oneself is a *topos*, a recurrent phrase, timeworn by literary usage. It did not have to be true, it had to fit.

Don Quichote, for instance, speaks of the two ways of acquiring wealth or glory: 'There are two paths, my daughters, to honour and wealth. One is the path of Letters, the other that of Arms. I myself have more arms than learning and I incline to arms, since I was born under Mars.' So he becomes a wanderer, poor as a church mouse and full of the most wonderful misapprehensions. Maestertius lived a less adventurous life, but his elected path earned him a successful professorship in Leiden and even an English knighthood.

The choice between words and weapons, *arte et marte*, is a literary theme stretching back to Homer. The greatness of Homer, wrote one seventeenth-century writer, was the way in which his two books reflected the two main options in human life: the *Iliad* represented the military life, and the *Odyssey* stood for civilian life. Again and again, literary critics pitted Achilles against Homer, the one a great general, the other a great poet, the man who actually performed glorious deeds as opposed to the man who preserved them for posterity.

Traditionally, these possibilities were viewed in one of two ways – as mutually antagonistic or as mutually enhancing. Plato wrote that a king must have strength and wisdom; *fortitudo* and *sapientia* are the qualities that define the ideal ruler. In his *Republic*, Plato wrote that only those who proved best in philosophy and with respect to war could be king. And the *imperator literatus* remained a constant figure in classical literature, a ruler who combined skill in weaponry with a knowledge of poetry and rhetoric, philosophy and music.

But all too often, this proved a fragile blend. Cicero's well-known half-verse *'cedant arma togae'* implies that the force of arms must yield to the rule of law, a sentiment echoed by Dousa's first epigrams. In Cicero's conviction that the Muses fall silent when weapons speak – *'inter arma silent musae'* – words and weapons are locked into emphatic antagonism: an opposition that the Middle Ages confirmed with the different status accorded nobles and clergy and the different associations linked to the use of arms and the pursuit of godliness.

The Christian culture complicated this opposition in a remarkable way. In the Old Testament, in the Book of Job, life on earth is compared to military service – in the text of the Vulgate, *'Militia est vita hominis super terram.'* Although there is nothing exclusively Christian about this military notion – the same comparison can be found in the early Stoics, in Plato's *Apology* and the writings of Seneca – this Christian soldier evolved into a carefully elaborated literary figure, who symbolised the struggle against the cruelty of nature and the darkness of sin.

Christianity thus increased the tension that had existed in the old contrast between weapons and words. Here again, two separate traditions can be distinguished. On the one hand, there was the fundamental dualism between God and the world, between *Civitas Dei* and the *civitas terrena*. On the other hand, a second distinction looms into view, between enduring the suffering of life, as embodied by the figure of Job, and the missionary activity characterised by Paul's epistles.

The opposition between arms and words was depicted in emblem books of

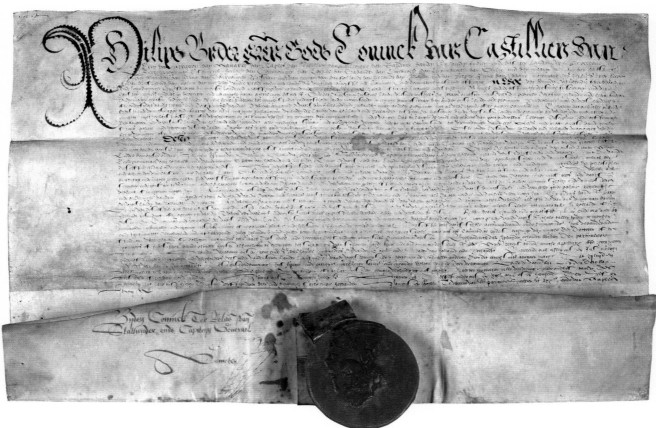

▲ *The university's foundation charter, dated 6 January 1575, issued in the name of King Philip II*

▲   *The Faliede Bagijnkerk, which served as the main university building from 1577 to 1581,*
     and later housed the library, Anatomy Theatre and fencing school

the Renaissance and later periods in a variety of ways: by the pen and the sword, weapons and the academic gown, book and spear, dagger and laurel wreath, lyre and trumpet. It was associated with a long line of philosophical and psychological associations: endurance and deeds, purity and promiscuity, theory and practice, *vita contemplativa* and *vita activa*. All of these are variations on the dualism with which Western culture was saturated. Up to a point, they were reconciled in the university, an institution that, in this form, was a pre-eminently Western invention.

Administrative Structure

The statutes of Leiden University, those of 1575 and the revised version of 1631, sought to strike a balance between the three parties involved, the States of Holland, the city of Leiden and the university. They provided for the appointment of three representatives of the States of Holland as 'Patrons, Governors or Supervisors of the University'. In this regard, Leiden University reflected the late-mediaeval trend in which universities were no longer supranational centres but institutions with close ties to governmental bodies and other secular authorities.

There were no clear guidelines for the appointment of these governors, but a consensus arose in the first fifty years that the first governor represented the nobles, and as such presided over the body as a whole; another one, elected from the Supreme Court or the Court of Holland, represented the judiciary; and a third, elected from the city council of one of Holland's larger cities, represented the central political power.

After 1635, the cities successfully secured the second governorship too for themselves, and from 1641 onwards it was almost always former burgomasters of Amsterdam, Haarlem, Dordrecht or Delft who were appointed to two of the three positions. In the eighteenth century, the appointment of a governor became part of the national system of political factions. The machinations regarding appointments between ruling elites sometimes went very far. Amsterdam and Haarlem actually tried to secure permanent seats on Leiden University's board of governors. The most influential governor of the eighteenth century, Bentinck, stated baldly that 'cabals and intrigues were all part of the game and those unwilling to take part in them achieved nothing'.

In general, governors were men who had proven their worth. Most of them had studied, most commonly at Leiden, and most commonly law, and boasted immense political and administrative experience. They included influential men such as François van Aerssen and Cornelis de Witt, Coenraad van Beuningen and Willem Bentinck, and great scholars such as Janus Dousa and Cor-

▲   *One of the earliest pictures of the Academiegebouw or main university building, taken from the* liber amicorum *of a Leiden law student*

nelis van der Mijle, Cornelis van Beveren and Hiëronymus van Beverninck. The prestige attached to a governorship of Leiden University can be inferred from the fact that even pensionaries of Holland such as Paulus Buys and Adriaen Pauw, Jacob Cats and Pieter Steyn held the post at various times. The highest-ranking official in the province, who, together with the *stadholder*, held supreme political power, did not consider it beneath his dignity, it seems, to accept a governorship of Leiden University and to attend the meetings of the governors with the burgomasters, five or six times a year.

Since the university had to be financed from the revenue of a number of former monasteries – most notably the Abbey of Egmond – the governors were assisted by a steward. A permanent secretary took care of the paperwork. Both of these officials were drawn from Leiden's elite and had generally been active in the city government. The combination of the position of steward or secretary with that of burgomaster was a frequent occurrence. A highly influential figure such as Johan van den Bergh had two sons-in-law who were appointed secretary. In the second case, the appointment was actually incorporated into the matrimonial contract.

The emphasis on equilibrium in the university's board of governors can also be inferred from the rule that the board must not be formed of three governors only, but that it must also include the city's four burgomasters. The fact that this gave the burgomasters a majority was offset by their limited term of office (just two years), while governors were appointed for life. Notwithstanding these checks and balances, the interaction between governors and burgomasters was a delicate affair. Clashes of interests or personal animosities sometimes strained their relations.

Ultimately, however, it was the States of Holland that wielded most power. It was their representatives, the governors, who played first fiddle. Until the city resigned itself to the authority of the States in 1594, the States also concerned themselves directly with the university. After that, they delegated their power to the governors, and only in extremely turbulent times, notably those caused by the religious crises of 1618 (Amenianism) and 1656 (Cartesianism), did they take the helm again.

Another delicate balance was that between the university's administra-

▲ *William I, Prince of Orange (1533-1584), with escutcheon*

▲ *Maurits, Prince of Orange (1567-1625), with escutcheon*

tors and the *stadholder*. William of Orange concerned himself deeply with 'his' university, but his son Maurits was also urged to get involved, for instance, in efforts to appoint famous professors such as Scaliger, Vorstius and Molinaeus. The special course for engineers that was launched in Leiden in 1600 was an idea initiated by Maurits. After the *wetsverzetting* (change of government) of 1618, every professorial appointment had to have his approval. The influence of *Stadholder* William III, who was respectfully known as the 'Highest Governor of this University', was comprehensive, but even the far weaker William IV proved to be extremely influential, partly through the generous funds he disbursed to the university and in 1750 by actually granting it complete dispensation from taxes.

The statutes have almost nothing to say about the relations that existed between the university's administrators (board of governors and burgomasters) and professors (the senate). The board of governors appointed professors and fixed their salaries. But there were a great many decisions that had to be taken jointly with the senate. The two bodies determined together, for instance, what subjects a new professor would teach and the overall structure of the curriculum. In all these matters, the board of governors had the last word, and only once, in 1593, in special circumstances – one governor had just died, another was on poor terms with the burgomasters, and a third was caught up in business at the Supreme Court in The Hague – did the Senate declare that the governors were superfluous and propose that the pensionary of Holland be appointed chancellor.

The proposal was not followed up, and after that, only questions of honour – the order in a procession, the seating at official dinners – would disrupt relations. The importance attached to such issues, and the indignation provoked by any breach of customary procedure, is clear from the fact that the burgomasters declined to attend the dinner held to celebrate the university's foundation day for eight years in a row after 1725, since in that year the rector had addressed the senate *before* the city's magistrates in his jubilee address.

Town and Gown

There was another bone of contention between town and university; the 'privileges', as they were known. Most of these were immunities, exemptions from the payment of taxes (toll charges, tax on beer and wine) or from performing certain services (having troops billeted in one's home, serving in the militia). They were granted by the city, albeit reluctantly and in an atmosphere of constant wrangling. The city complained that the university admitted too many people, who enrolled only to take advantage of the fiscal exemptions. It was only a matter of time, someone observed dryly in 1582, before everyone in the town had signed up at the university.

This problem was as old as the university itself. The requirement that every student enrol had actually been introduced, as the faculty of humanities in Paris had put it in 1289, because it was impossible to distinguish between 'those who are good and regular students, and those who are not genuine and who pretend to be studying at our Faculty in order to enjoy the associated privileges and freedoms.' 'Spurious students and other hangers-on' should be removed as 'good-for-nothings … from the bosom and the organisation of the faculty'.

Leiden's student registration lists demonstrate the complexity of the problem: the 'hangers-on' frequently did have ties of some kind with the university. Entire households were placed on the tax collector's list; but then it was not uncommon for the family to accompany the son to a university town. Petrus Doorninck, for instance, a 'man of letters' who registered on 27 March 1650, mentioned his children's upbringing explicitly as a reason for enrolling: *'alens hic liberos suos'*. And every year the new rector would register ten to twenty boys, frequently aged between 12 and 15, who were pupils of the Latin School. The top two classes of this school were entitled to register at the university. Although the line between school and university was drawn quite clearly in the course of the seventeenth century, the fact that these pupils had the same entitlements as students reflects the traditionally blurred distinction between the two.

All sorts of officials also registered, not only those directly connected to the university, like beadles and porters, but also administrators and servants (*famuli*) of students and various individuals with some connection to student life, such as those who taught fencing, dancing, French, Italian, art and music. A lengthy report dating from 1750, drawn up by the rector and intended to put an end to these practices, lists countless artistic and technical occupations, including draughtsmen and painters, engravers and mathematicians, surveyors and all kinds of instrument-makers. Added to this, of course, are all the local surgeons and apothecaries and their students, the town physicians, local lawyers, soldiers, church wardens and postmasters, secretaries of country estates, Protestant ministers and even – but that is because we are now some way into the eighteenth century – Catholic priests and journalists.

There also appears to have been a brisk trade in tax exemptions. Foreign students in particular, who stayed for only a few months while their exemptions were granted for a whole year, avidly traded in these privileges. The German chronicler of student life Friedrich Luca wrote about his stay in Leiden: 'One can also easily sell such Privileges to a burgher, which many others and indeed I myself have done'. Professors too saw the lucrative side of tax exemptions. In 1613, the board of governors convened a meeting of the Senate to discuss the grave accusations of the wine tax farmers, 'that the professors had recorded [the consumption of] so much wine that they were suspected of certain villainous practices'.

By far the most important privilege was the Forum Privilegiatum, the university's own tribunal. All those registered in the Album Studiosorum, not just students, were entitled to put their case to this body, whether as plaintiff or defendant. This custom originated from the days of the famous privilege for scholars studying law, the Authentica Habita, which was issued by order of Frederick Barbarossa at the Reichstag of Roncaglia in 1158. It protected foreign students and authorised them to go where they pleased, 'so that all those who wish to study are free to come and go and stay in liberty.'

The existence of such a court obviously undermined the competence of other local tribunals. And since it was more than probable that most of the cases it heard would relate to problems that arose between students and local townspeople, the city of Leiden demanded and obtained an important vote in

IANVS DOVSA, NOORTWICI TOPARCHA, V. G.

Ex Imagine V.N.
Iani Dousa ad
Vivum Pickt.

Non solùm DVLCES virtus Nordwicia MVSAS,
Omnia sed Mavors quæ sibi poscit, habet.
Cui studium patrijs arcere penatibus hostem_.:
Auraicoque datam non temerare fidem_.

Nec satis Heroi, Martem sperare secundum_;
Pugnat, & Aonias sperat in urbe deas,
Principis invicti donum_. Procul ite profani;
Hic sacer est, Dousa conciliante, locus.

Corn. Visscher sculpsit
Petro Soutmanno
dirigente et
excudente
Harlemi 1649.

PETRVS SCRIVERIVS.

Cum Privilegio.

▲ *Janus Dousa (Jan van den Does) (1545-1604), first curator of the university (1575-1604)*

the tribunal. The senate was represented, in hearings, by the rector and four assessors attached to the faculties. The four burgomasters and two magistrates represented the city. Furthermore, the city's sheriff acted as *promotor* or public prosecutor.

The university was very keen to retain this privilege. The case against a Catholic schoolteacher, in 1587, proved to be crucial. This Willem van Assendelft offered accommodation to students and was accused of instructing those in his charge 'in the Jesuit catechism as promulgated by Petrus Canisius'. As soon as the Senate heard that the Court of Holland had brought these charges, it applied for them to be dismissed and even forbade Van Assendelft to appear before the Court of Holland, on penalty of having his university

▲   *Great Seal of the university*

privileges withdrawn. A hearing of the university's own tribunal was hurriedly convened, at which Van Assendelft was acquitted. The tribunal did order him, however, not to teach anything that conflicted with the Protestant religion. The Court of Holland also heard the case, thus generating some fantastically theatrical scenes and an immense bureaucratic tangle. Eventually the States of Holland decided to dismiss the case, and to recognise Leiden's special privileges. The university would defend itself against any infringement of its rights until the end of the eighteenth century by invoking the precedent of the Assendelft case and the resolution adopted by the States of Holland.

That is not to say that the privileges were never challenged. Problems with the Court of Holland, with the various courts in the province, and with the more independent students continued to occur. The most important issues, however, were those in which the city was pitted against the university. The presence in the city of students from different backgrounds, both social and regional, gave rise to substantial problems of interpretation. Those from different countries – most notably the Germans, but the French and English as well – had different customs and codes of conduct. Furthermore, there was a certain social tension between the local population, which was mainly Protestant and worked in the cloth industry, and the student population, which was diverse in terms of religion and primarily upper-class.

On 9 February 1600, a number of representatives '*ex ordine Studiosi Leidenses*' wrote to the board of governors demanding protection and referring explicitly to the *Authentica Habita*. They refused to be subject to a completely 'licentious night watch', as they put it, nor would they tolerate being treated on an equal footing with people they described as catamites and rag-and-bone men, sutlers and apprentice barbers. They also protested adamantly against the constant abuse hurled at foreign students, for instance the habit of jeering '*mofmaff, mofmaff*!' [an early form of *mof* = approx. *kraut*, transl.] at the German students.

The situation culminated in a shocking incident in 1607, when a law student who was celebrating a successful end of a disputation was shot dead, with 21 bullets, in the presence of his professor. According to the professor,

▲   *Jan van Hout (1542-1609), secretary of the board of governors (1575-1596)*

the famous jurist Everard Bronchorst, who recorded the events in his diary, the students had been guilty of nothing but 'merry laughter'. The leader of the night watch maintained that the aggression of the students, who had wanted to take their revenge for earlier confrontations, forced the militiamen to defend themselves.

The incident led to the founding of a special student militia, over fifty man strong, which was better trained and under more judicious command than the regular civic guard. Its mandate was to guarantee safety in the streets, in close cooperation with the senate. This night watch was a compromise solution agreed between the States of Holland and the city of Leiden, who paid for it jointly. The detailed instructions issued to this student police laid down exactly what was seen as a breach of the law and how students should be treated. If a student was arrested, a full report had to be submitted to the rector and/or burgomaster the next morning.

The existence of such joint institutions demonstrates the university's special position in the city. And although these bodies solved some problems, they created others. The city soon asserted its right to appoint the leaders of the student police. The university agreed to preserve the peace, just as it caved in later, in 1652, when the city demanded the right to appoint the secretary of the university tribunal. Five years later, the city council summoned Professor Thysius to the town hall to explain why he had dared to publish a book with the words 'Hollandse Academie', 'Academia Batava' (Academy of Holland, Academy of Batavia) on the title page, where it should have read 'Academia Lugduno-Batava', meaning Academy of Leiden. The senate immediately protested to the States of Holland that the city was trying to steal 'one of the greatest powers vested in any sovereign'.

This also prompted the senate to investigate the precise division of powers between board of governors and burgomasters. In April 1658, a list of seventeen grievances was presented to the pensionary of Holland, regarding infringements of the university's privileges. The burgomasters attended senate meetings or failed to attend as it suited them, and summoned not only regular professors but even the rector to appear. They had demanded the appointment of a number of university officials, secretaries and beadles. They removed the names of people they knew from the enrolment registers and assigned university privileges to people not entitled to them. They compelled professors to provide accommodation to all sorts of people and to contribute to the funding of the city's infrastructure. What is more, they had imprisoned, aggrieved and offended members of the University, 'many of whom were princes, dukes, nobles and the ablest men in the land'.

In their defence, the burgomasters emphasised that they were inseparable from the board of governors, but that was precisely what the senate disputed. Article 3 of the Statutes provided that the senate must seek the advice of the board of governors on 'matters that were weighty and of great consequence'. What could be more important than the university's privileges, and what was more nonsensical than to seek the advice of the opposing party? They proposed that article 3 be reworded, such that only the actual board of governors should be asked for its advice, 'excluding the burgomasters'. But the States of Holland opted for vagueness rather than clarity, and for constant adjustments to the rules instead of a clear definition of the respective areas of competence.

The Recruitment of Professors

The appointment of new professors, as we have seen, was the shared responsibility of the board of governors and the burgomasters. But other parties too were involved. Outside the university, these included not only members of the House of Orange, but also the synod of the Reformed Church. Other non-official political or cultural groups also tried to sway decisions to suit their own agendas. In addition, the university authorities consulted leading professors at home and prominent diplomats and intellectuals abroad. Lipsius and Scaliger, Rivet and Salmasius were all asked with some frequency to propose candidates or to mediate in negotiations.

Sometimes the incumbent professor was asked to nominate possible successors. More often, the advice was sought, generally on an informal level, of the faculty, the dean, or a distinguished professor. The diary kept by Bronchorst, professor of law from 1587 to 1621, documents regular exchanges between the board of governors and the faculty when new appointments were being considered. Sometimes the entire senate was asked for its advice, and in 1620 its members made an unsuccessful bid to get their say in such matters written into the statutes.

The appointments policy that developed in the university's first hundred years was also a question of equilibrium. In the first place, there was the need to strike the right balance between established reputation and youthful promise. From the outset, governors used the name and fame of a few renowned intellectuals to compensate for the fact that no one in Europe had ever heard of their new institution. The aim, no doubt, was to put out bait to attract other great scholars. They therefore appointed a number of *honorarii*, as they were called. The first were Justus Lipsius and Hugo Donellus. Janus Dousa saw it as his finest achievement that he had given the new and insignificant university its first celebrity, with the appointment of Lipsius. 'We well recall how small and obscure was the university at the time of your arrival,' recalled the governors when Lipsius left in 1591, 'as we recall how, and through whose actions and policy, it has since grown, matured and acquired its own distinctive character'.

The success of Lipsius's appointment led to others, such as those of Carolus Clusius and Josephus Justus Scaliger in 1593 and Claudius Salmasius in 1632. They earned two or three times as much as the other professors, and yet they were not in fact professors at all, in the narrowest sense of the term. They did not attend meetings of the senate, they were not required to give lectures, and their names did not appear in the *Series Lectionum*. The inscription on the portrait of Scaliger that was hung above his bequest in the university library stated that he was *'decus Academiae'*, not a professor but an 'ornament' of the university.

But fame was expensive, and the university compensated for such outlays by purchasing promise, which cost considerably less. Not just for financial reasons, but also in order to choose from a small pool of young and promising scholars, who had frequently only just graduated, the governors created the possibility of teaching 'to gain experience' (*'experiundi causa'*). This was no new idea; young men who had gained their doctorates at the great humanities

► *Designs for beadle's staffs, c. 1594*

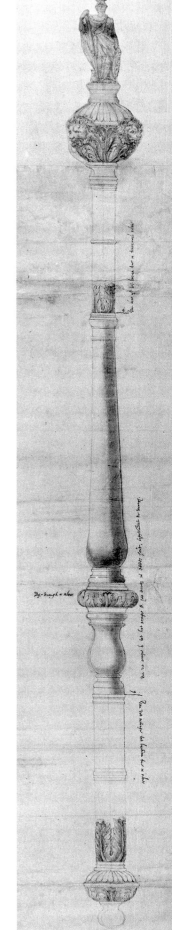

faculties of Paris and Oxford had originally been required to stay on and teach there for a few years. Mediaeval universities also distinguished between 'ordinary' and 'extraordinary' lecturers, whereby the latter lectured on minor texts to younger students.

Leiden University did not pay for these lectures by promising young scholars. The idea was to give them the opportunity to demonstrate their aptitude for teaching and hence their suitability for a professorship. Competitive demonstrations were sometimes organised, in which three or four young men came forward to display their abilities. In 1599, when one professor of philosophy remained, as many as five students were assigned lecturing duties: Bertius, Bontius, Murdison, Vossius and Heurnius, all of whom eventually secured professorships. Contests of this kind occasionally led to dual appointments, with two young men being obliged to share a professor's meagre starting salary, as happened first in 1597, when Swanenburch and Pynacker were appointed jointly to the professorship in law.

As far as the middle ranks of lecturers were concerned, the governors scrutinised the course of their studies and their practical experience more than their scholarly output. In Leiden University's first hundred years, its professors had attended an average of two or three universities – 2.7 to be precise – two-thirds of which were outside the Republic. German institutions were the most common, followed by those of Paris and Orléans. Professors of the medical faculty still inclined towards universities in Italy. Over the following century, the academic horizon of Leiden's professors narrowed somewhat. At the end of this period they had attended an average of two universities (more precisely 1.9), three-quarters of which were in the United Provinces.

Aspiring professors would generally have studied for at least six years, followed by an average of ten years' practical experience – generally in line with their studies – before being appointed to a chair in Leiden. Some 30 per cent of the university's professors had previously held a chair at another university. There was only one exception to this strong preference for experienced teachers: when someone was assigned to teaching duties immediately after completing his studies, he was almost invariably the son of a professor.

◄ *Sculpture representing Lady Justice from the Academic Tribunal, 1653*

In the eighteenth century, the transition from another profession to a professorship in Leiden took place increasingly by way of a professorship elsewhere. And in that second century, one-third of Leiden's professors had only academic experience.

The Senate

The first statutes provided that the *corpus* of the university consisted not only of rector and professors, but also of 'the Doctors and *Magistri* who have graduated from that university and have their residence there'. In 1587, Lipsius insisted that 'even for those who are not professors', this provision must be firmly implemented. But there is no indication that any Leiden graduate ever attended a senate meeting. Meetings took place at irregular intervals and were presided over by the rector.

The rector was elected, generally for a year at a time, by the *stadholder* (or by the States in stadholderless periods) from a list of three names of professors, a list drawn up each February by the senate. The city's burgomasters had to approve the nominations, but the *stadholder* had the last word. The only formal requirement for the position of rector was the ability to speak Dutch. And this was only invoked when convenient. In the case of the greatly respected Donellus it does not seem to have worried anyone that he did not speak a word of Dutch. But when the supercilious Drelincourt put himself forward, language suddenly became a barrier, in spite of Drelincourt's insistence that his Dutch was excellent.

In the beginning, the choice of a rector was determined primarily by a professor's authority among his fellows. Lipsius and A.E. Vorstius were each elected four times, Cornelis de Groot and Johannes Heurnius six times, and Polyander a record eight times. But the new statutes of 1631 determined that after serving for a term, a rector would have to wait four years before he could be appointed again. The same restriction applied to the faculty from which the rector had been drawn. Thus, a rotating system developed, in which seniority became the main criterion for a faculty's nomination.

▲ *William of Orange, depicted as the Father of the Nation and a soldier of Christ*

▲   *Thomas Erpenius (1584-1624), professor of Arabic and Oriental Languages (1613-1624)*

Aside from chairing senate meetings, the rector's main task was to represent the university in the outside world. He had frequent contact with the burgomaster and often went to The Hague to attend sessions of the States. He also had to hold high the university's honour, receive ambassadors and other important guests, offer help to impecunious students and arrange facilities for itinerant scholars. And besides all this, of course, he had to take care of the students, enrol them and ensure compliance with regulations.

The rector was assisted by four representatives of the faculties known as assessors, two of whom were replaced each February. Together they formed a body whose main task was to decide, together with the board of governors, which subjects the new professors should teach. They could do so quite precisely, by designating a particular book or explanation, but more frequently the professor's teaching mandate would be defined in fairly vague terms. And appointees could – and did – bend the rules. Dominicus Baudius, having professed his aversion to a particular rhetorical address by Cicero, was permitted to teach something closer to his heart instead, an ode by Pliny.

The senate was not permitted to grow beyond a certain maximum size. The statutes of 1575 allowed for eleven full professors, while those of 1631 allowed for fifteen at most. 'Extraordinary' professors were not entitled to attend senate meetings. The senate had good reason to keep to its maximum limit, since the revenue from enrolments and disputations was divided among the members. But here too, balance played a role. When Henricus Bornius was appointed professor of philosophy in 1654, the senate protested, arguing that there were already sixteen professors and that the philosophy faculty already had six. If Bornius were appointed, there would be 'more professors in the lowest faculty than in the main faculties of theology and law.'

The ranking order of the faculties in Leiden, as elsewhere, was a source of constant problems within the senate. The difference in hierarchy was a question of tradition and was reflected in the *Series Lectionum*. When different professors lectured at the same time, the theologian was listed first, then the jurist or physician, and lastly the philosopher. Full professors were always listed before extraordinary appointees. This may seem perfectly plain and simple, but in practice countless problems arose, especially when similar

subjects were taught at the same time, or when subjects were not clearly defined. Supplementary private lectures taught by professors also provoked
heated debate.

Differences in background and origin also gave rise to misunderstandings. In Leiden University's first twenty years, foreign professors were in the
majority. In its first century, over one-third (37 to 44 per cent) of the university's professors, most of them theologians and philosophers, came from
abroad. Of these, the majority (32 in total, over one-fifth), came from the
Southern Netherlands, but there were also ten from France. Before 1650 there
was only a handful of Germans, but their numbers steadily increased after
that.

The differences in social background, too, were very considerable. Most
of Leiden's professors were from the upper middle classes: the exact proportion varied from one faculty to the next, ranging from 73 (law) to 86 per cent
(humanities). But 20 per cent of theology professors and as many as 25 per
cent of professors of medicine boasted a still more distinguished, patrician
background. Then there were the religious differences. In the first few decades of the university's existence, recognised libertines such as Lipsius and
Vulcanius, Raphelengius and Erpenius (Thomas van Erpe) rubbed shoulders
with radical Calvinists such as Danaeus (Lambert Daneau) and Saravia. The
professors even included staunch Catholics such as Sosius and Tuning.

After the change of government of 1618 – the result of Maurits's victory
over Oldenbarneveldt and of strict Calvinism over free-thinking Protestants
– this religious diversity disappeared, and Leiden became almost exclusively
Calvinist. The appointment of a Lutheran always provoked debate, and the
Mennonite Golius had to become a Calvinist. Other differences became less
distinct. Leiden professorships became more national in the university's second century. Still, somewhere between a quarter and a third of appointees
still came from abroad, primarily from Germany. Most of them taught law,
transforming the law faculty from the most national into the most international faculty in the university; conversely, the theology faculty became primarily national. Almost all of the professors now came from the upper middle
classes, and fewer from trade and bureaucracy, as compared to the seven-

▲ *Hugo de Groot (1583-1645), graduate of Leiden University*

▲ *Simon Stevin (1548-1620), who devised the Nederduitsche Mathematique (1600),*
   the first course in applied science in the Netherlands

teenth century, but more from the scholarly professions.

There were other factors that kneaded Leiden's initially diverse and some-times sharply divided body of professors into a more unified whole. Leaving aside the rector's repeated exhortations to behave like good Christians and learned colleagues, the professorial peace was preserved by regular commu-nal feasts. The first time such a feast was proposed was in 1580. They grew in-to rituals, held first once and soon twice a year, in summer and winter. In the eighteenth century, other meals were added, such as the *convivium aditiale* that each new professor would host for his colleagues, and the feast held to celebrate a professor's 25th anniversary in that position.

Certain other rituals also fostered unity in the senate. The inaugural ad-dress, a practice that evolved from the first address given by a mediaeval doc-tor, gradually became an ingrained custom. About half of Leiden's professors launched their new career in this way in the latter half of the seventeenth century, and after 1700 virtually every freshly appointed professor did so. By then this address was regarded as the official moment at which the new pro-fessor entered into office. It gave him an opportunity, as Boerhaave put it when he took up his chair in chemistry in 1718, 'to point out the benefits of its commended qualities and at the same time to encourage diligence among the students.'

Along with the entrenchment of this official ceremony came a trend for professors to don their robes of office more frequently. From 1677 onwards professors were fined for appearing at public Ph.D. ceremonies without their robes, and two years later the requirement was extended to cover attendance at funerals. From 1730 onwards, professors were even encouraged to wear their robes at private Ph.D. formalities (*non nisi palliati*). At the same time, the right to wear a robe (*ius togae*) was defined more precisely. The sheriff was permitted to wear one on since he sat on the university tribunal, but church ministers who did so were deemed to be acting against established custom.

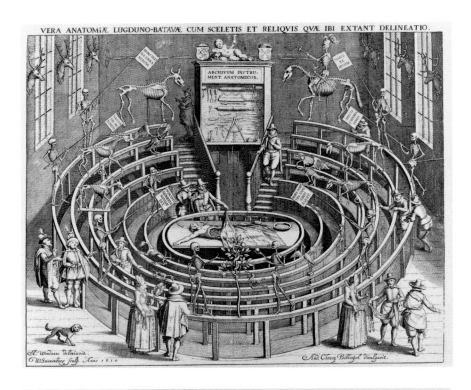

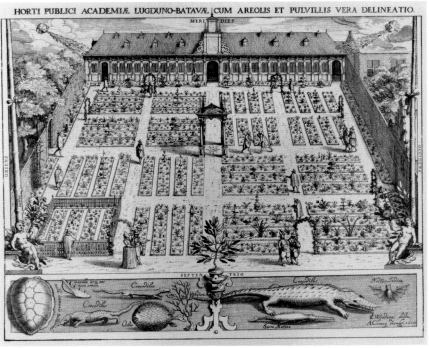

▲ *Anatomy Theatre, 1610*
▼ *Botanical Gardens, 1610*

BIBLIOTHECÆ. LUGDUNO-BATAVÆ. CUM PULPITIS ET ARCIS VERA IXNOGRAPHIA.

DELINEATIO LVDI PVBLICI GLADIATORII VRBIS ET ACADEMIÆ LVGDVNENSIS APVD BATAVOS.

▲ *Library, 1610*
▼ *Fencing School, 1610*

Dogma and Equilibrium

The most common causes of strife in the senate were probably 'ideological' in nature. In 1665, for instance, at a senate meeting culminating in a debate about Descartes, De Raei defended the position of radical doubt – that is, doubt even where there was no specific reason for it, such as in the case of the existence of the human spirit or of God. When Cocceius (Johannes Coch), whose rational theology was often taken for Cartesianism, referred to this position as paradoxical and said that the Cartesians had fewer doubts than they claimed, De Raei retorted: 'You are a philosophical nonentity!'

Heated debates resulted in part from a peculiarity of the university's personnel policy. The governors did their best to strike a balance between the different ideological, philosophical and scholarly trends of the day. Most notably in theology and philosophy, opposing dogmas could provoke fierce arguments and in some cases political unrest. Even so, in 1603, the board of governors appointed not only the latitudinarian Arminius but also the orthodox Calvinist Trelcatius Junior, and in 1611 not only Conrad Vorstius but also Petrus Molinaeus. In 1650 they appointed Cocceius alongside Trigland, in 1653 Hoornbeek alongside Cocceius.

So, whenever the board appointed someone with moderate views, they deliberately sought a countervailing force in the form of a more 'precise', more dogmatic thinker. In philosophy, this led to the appointment of different varieties of Aristotelianism: Gilbert Jack as well as Petri Burgersdijk, Adam Stuart as well as Adriaan Heereboord, and Adam Stuart's son David as well as Johannes de Raei. Since the humanities would gradually occupy the centre ground at Leiden University, the kind of Aristotelianism that was cultivated by the young university merits further consideration.

The Scottish philosopher Gilbert Jack was a typical exponent of the early Leiden Aristotelianism, in the sense that he was a fairly loyal follower of the Jesuit Francisco Suárez, including Suárez's compromise between natural theology and Christian revelation. This may seem surprising given the Protestant setting, but Aristotelian ideas provided the common ground; the Jesuit's influence was also clearly discernible in the ideas of Jack's younger colleague Petri Burgersdijk. The latter, however, while taking natural theology as his point of departure, judiciously maintained a strict distinction between theology and philosophy.

The States of Holland subsequently gave this position the official stamp of approval in an *Ordre* prohibiting the mixing of theology and philosophy. This ruling seemed at the time to be a compromise, designed to prevent philosophical arguments being invoked in theological questions, but as time went on it proved to have the converse effect, safeguarding philosophy from the interventions of theology.

No less eclectic was Burgersdijk in his natural philosophy. In the field of astronomy he dealt with Copernicanism as well as the Ptolemaic world view. He mentioned the arguments of Philippus van Lansbergen, a follower of Copernicus, and emphasised their plausibility. But he refused to concede that these arguments undermined the Aristotelian line of reasoning. The same applied to his pupil, the consummate eclectic Adriaan Heereboord. Although he tried to break away from the Jesuits' influence and sought to develop a Protestant metaphysics in which an innate light compels human beings to acknowledge God's existence, Heereboord remained within the bounds of Aristotelian thought. Towards the end of his life he even tried to reconcile Aristotle with Descartes.

The next step away from pure Aristotelianism in the direction of a more empirical approach to science was taken by Johannes de Raei, the only true Cartesian ever to occupy a chair at Leiden. His *Clavis philosophiae naturalis* (1654) was intended as 'an introduction to the Aristotelian-Cartesian view of nature' (*Introductio ad naturae contemplationem Aristotelico-Cartesiana*). In what appeared to be a traditional mixture, a *philosophia novantiqua*, De Raei reversed the old order and tied the ideas he wanted to retain from Aristotle to a Cartesian thread. Equally original was the way in which he set philosophy apart from theology: by stressing the contemplative nature of philosophy and by distinguishing between the practical and the strictly theoretical.

An important conclusion can be distilled from all this. The university evidently succeeded not only in allowing different schools of thought to be expressed in the curriculum, but also in keeping their internal disputes under control. Even in cases of unmitigated polemic division – as in different forms of Aristotelianism or relations between Aristotelianism and Cartesianism – Leiden's university learning proved to be defined primarily as a quest for eclectic compromise or gradual transition.

And for any scholars who perhaps lacked a natural inclination to conform to this intention, there were statutes exhorting them to do so. Adam Stuart and his son David were contemporaneous representatives of conservative Aristotelianism. To keep them in check, the board of governors had instructed them to discuss Aristotle's text as literally as possible – that is, word for word. This too proved to be an excellent way of nipping philosophical debate in the philological bud.

The university continued this appointments policy in the second century of its existence. For instance, Wolferd Senguerd was appointed alongside the Cartesian Burchardus de Volder as professor 'in peripatetic Philosophy ... the better to preserve continuity'. And although Senguerd remained faithful to the Aristotelian, qualitative concepts of matter and form, he defined form as matter in motion, and matter itself, with Descartes, as extension. Wanting both to give Cartesianism its due and to abide by a qualitative mode of reasoning, he solved the problem by focusing on experimental science. It was around the same time that De Volder, just back from a trip to England where he had attended a meeting of the Royal Society, asked the board of governors to give him a mandate as 'Professor Physicae experimentalis'.

Thus, Senguerd and De Volder effectively followed the instructions that had been given to the Stuarts: they avoided controversy by concentrating, in this case, not on the text but on reality. But what for the Stuarts had been pure conservatism was in this case wholly innovative. The moderate Aristotelian Senguerd and the equally moderate Cartesian De Volder joined forces in the first physics laboratory in the Northern Netherlands, where they gave the first series of lectures based entirely on experiments. In so doing, they initiated a complete educational revolution: for their successors Boerhaave, 's Gravesande and Van Musschenbroek, experiments were the linchpin of their teaching. Experiments not only enabled them to eschew speculation and conflicts of dogma, but also restored the old unity between philosophy and theol-

▶ *Egyptian antiquities from the Anatomy Theatre*

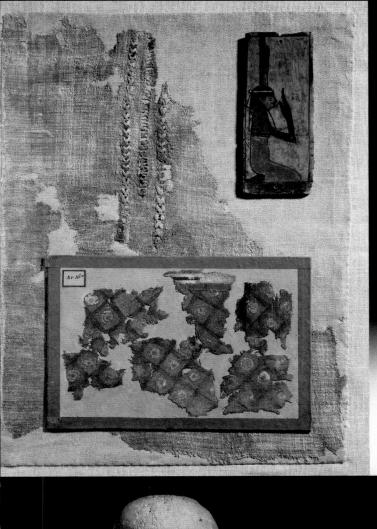

▲ *Panorama of Constantinople, displayed on the north wall of the library from 1598 onwards*

ogy – paving the way for what became known as physico-theology, *The wisdom of God manifested in the works of creation*, to borrow the title of John Ray's influential book.

These changes made themselves felt throughout the curriculum. Logic, which had been the most important subject in philosophy, gave way to natural philosophy, while syllogisms gave way to reasoning by analogy. Whether one wished to compare culture to a language, the physiology of plants to human sexuality, chemical processes to human emotions, or the diversity of legal reality to the rationalism of Roman law, the analogy proved a wonderfully versatile tool. Provided certain conditions were met, it helped to reformulate the unknown in terms of what was known, and to clarify reality by using rational or ideal-typical models.

The emphasis on striking a balance between dogmas was not confined to theology and philosophy. The different *mores* were represented in law and medicine too: a more philological school coexisted with a more practical one, a more systematic interpretation with a more chronological one, a more encyclopaedic mode of teaching with a more experimental one. The way the board of governors went about finding a suitable successor to the physician Johan Antonides van der Linden provides a good example.

Van der Linden was a devout follower of Hippocrates. While his immediate colleagues Franciscus Sylvius (Franz de la Boë) and Johannes Hornius were scientists by training – both known for their empirical research, in which one sought to establish the composition of bodily fluids and the other the way in which these fluids were transported around the body – Van der Linden was a conservative, more encyclopaedic teacher. He did not deny that blood circulated – he even praised William Harvey as one who could not be praised sufficiently (*'nunquam satis laudatum'*) but he still maintained that Hippocrates had been the first to discover the phenomenon.

But Van der Linden had been an influential teacher, and Dutch envoys in England and France were asked to look out for a physician who drew on 'the old ways of Galen'. Ambassador Meerman in England suggested the names of Thomas Willis and even Robert Boyle. There was also one Ludovicus Molinaeus, who had recently published a book entitled *Medicina universalis Ga-*

lenica. He was sixty years of age, but had a young wife, and since his father had lived to a ripe age, Meerman assumed that Molinaeus had another thirty years of service in him. But Willis was not interested, Boyle was far too wealthy, and Molinaeus's prestige was found wanting. The Oxford dons George Castle and Carolo Offredi, an unmarried but Protestant physician in Padua, were thought to be more suitable candidates. However, eventually it was Charles Drelincourt – *Medicus Regis*, personal physician to the king of France, as he styled himself – who, having been found conservative enough, was offered the chair and agreed to accept it.

With a recruitment policy like this, controversy was obviously unavoida-

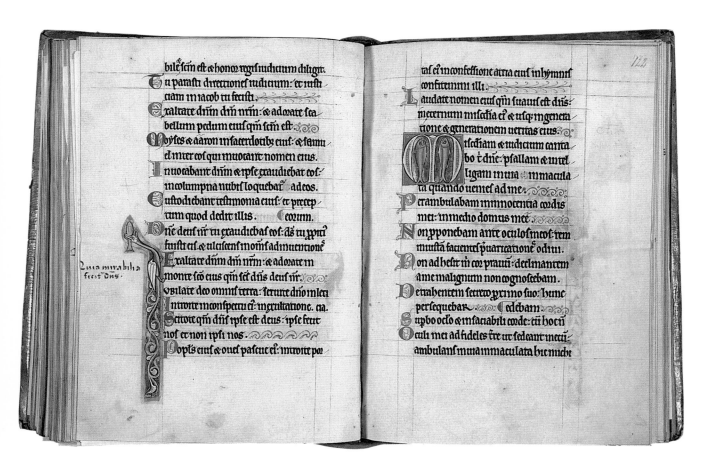

▲ *Psalter belonging to Louis IX of France (1214-1270), presented to the library
by Johan van den Bergh, burgomaster of Leiden*

ble. Such clashes were significant for three reasons: first, they fuelled the constant debate on fundamental scientific principles, such as systematic versus empirical knowledge, or mechanical versus organic explanations. Second, since they almost always exerted a certain influence on theological and political problems, they served as a kind of conductor, not preventing the lightning of debate from striking, but generally bringing it under control. And third, in this way, the university functioned as a kind of guide for the baffled, an intellectual information service that translated the great issues of the day into intelligible, accessible language.

A good example – one of many – of the way this mechanism operated is

▲ *Psalter belonging to Louis IX*

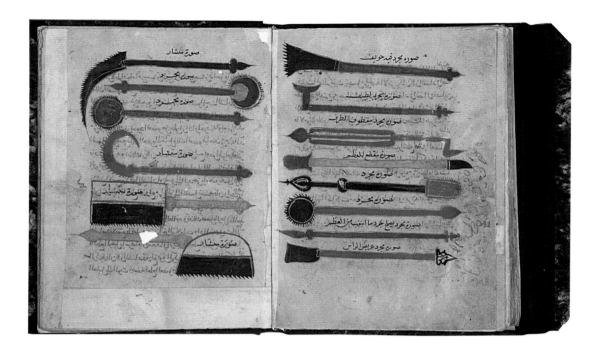

the 'hair war', a controversy about men with long hair. Calvinist ministers viewed long hair on men as a sign of the intemperance of the times, and they fervently lamented the passing of a more sober age. The Spanish Inquisition had killed only the body, but now French manners were murdering the soul. At the Provincial synod of 1640, the *classis* (Church governing body) of The Hague placed the subject on the agenda, and from the synod the subject made its way to the pulpit, where ministers admonished their congregations with I Corinthians 11:14: 'Doth not even nature itself teach you, that, if a man have long hair, it is a shame unto him?'. Vestries resounded with rhetoric, ministers threatened each other with dismissal, and the population lived in fear of war, the plague, or – worse still – higher prices.

In Leiden, the first to enter the fray were Boxhorn and Salmasius. The former published directly in Dutch. In his *Spiegeltien vertoonende 't lanck hayr ende hayrlocken, by de oude Hollandse ende Zeelanders gedragen* ('"Mirror" showing the long hair and locks as worn by the ancient men of Holland and Zeeland', 1644) he mainly sought to place the subject in its historical con-

▲ *Fourteenth-century manuscript with surgical instruments from the Middle East*

text. The Batavians had worn their hair long, he wrote, and since then it had become so common that it was almost a mark of national pride. In another treatise dating from the same year, he showed that short hair was in fact 'of foreign origin'.

The 747-page *Epistola ad Andream Colvium* that was translated into Dutch in 1644, was typical of Salmasius: a bewildering, all-encompassing chaos spread with earnest erudition. He omitted not a single hairstyle, kind of wearer, commentator, class or culture from his mountain of allusions, under the aegis of just one argument: that there were two sorts of apostolic commandments, namely those that possessed universal validity and those that were linked to a specific time or place. Paul's words about hair clearly belonged to the second category. Salmasius was supported not only by the ageing, moderate thinker Polyander, whose *Judicium* was approved by the theology faculty, but even by the strict Calvinist Revius, who devoted six disputations to the subject. In the end, the moderate voice of Leiden prevailed.

Debates of this kind clearly show the role that the university played in public opinion and in the forming of political and social views. Leiden University was never as intensively involved in public administration or the dispensation of justice as its German counterpart – *Aktenversendung* (the referral of a case for advisory opinions) – was unknown here. Even so, the professors were nonetheless fairly active in rendering services to society. Religious debate – whether erudite as with the Jews or disputatious as with the Catholics – was seen as an essential part of the professors' theological work, as was advising on certain books or controversies. The law faculty was frequently consulted in an official capacity, for matters ranging from matrimony between blood relatives to cases of extortionate interest, disturbances of the peace, land leasing, wills, rights of ownership, piracy and privateering. The other faculties fulfilled similar services. For instance, the medical and philosophical faculties responded jointly in 1594 to a question put to them by the Court of Holland. The Court wanted to know whether a woman who had been hurled into the water and who continued to float did so through witchcraft or natural powers. Both faculties concluded on the grounds of logical and empirical considerations that such 'trials by water' provided no legal evidence whatsoever.

Humanist Didactics

The academic year, though not long, was highly compressed. There was no regular teaching on Wednesdays or Saturdays, and besides the many holidays – generally two weeks each for Easter, Whitsuntide and Christmas and six weeks in the summer – many lectures were cancelled during book auctions, anatomy lessons, and major annual fairs. In the main, this left scarcely more than 160 to 170 days for lectures.

Lectures were divided into public and private classes. The former were open to all students registered at the university, free of charge. They were taught on all weekdays barring Wednesdays and Saturdays, which were reserved for private classes, demonstration lectures by *lectores* hoping to impress enough to secure a salaried appointment, and disputations. From 1587 onwards, posters were hung up each year on 1 October and 1 March, a *Series Lectionum* with the details of the regular timetable. Each professor would be scheduled to lecture for four hours in the week, on one or at most two subjects.

The university's large quotient of 'alternative' teaching was provided mainly by private individuals teaching in their own homes. They enrolled at the university and taught a wide range of subjects that sometimes overlapped with material covered by the professors, besides numerous supplementary classes ranging from fencing and horseback riding, singing and dancing, to French and Italian, draughtsmanship and arithmetic. But professors too taught private classes of this kind. The senate tried to curb this practice, but neither the professors nor lecturers from outside the senate took much notice. Predictably, time spent teaching these lucrative private classes led to the neglect of regular lectures. Even so, private classes became entrenched in everyday teaching practices, and indeed grew into usurping cuckoos, driving public lectures off the curriculum.

When one recalls that students not only came from different educational backgrounds, but came and went as they pleased – there was no prescribed overall course of study – the curriculum and the teaching based on it were remarkably coherent. This coherence was forged by trial and error, adjustment

▲ *Illustrations from the* Académie de l'espée *by Girard Thibault (1628)*

▲   *The four temperaments, prints from the collection of the Anatomy Theatre*

and ingenuity. The curriculum acquired its most essential traits in the early seventeenth century, foremost among which was undoubtedly that as a rule, Leiden's teaching adhered faithfully to the fundamental rules of humanist didactics.

These rules arose from a mixture of substantive, methodological and normative considerations. A good command of Latin and a certain familiarity with classical texts were needed to follow the lectures. Students were also expected to have mastered the elementary principles of logic, to be capable of thinking and reasoning methodically. These abilities were tested, and any blanks were taken into account, as far as possible, in the choice of subjects and their treatment.

A university student was thus expected to master a number of skills. He had to be able to distil and explain the 'argument' of a text, its structure, and the gist and consequences of a particular line of reasoning. He had to have his knowledge at the ready, stored in his memory or in a kind of scholarly apparatus. Finally, he had to be able to use his skills for the benefit of Church and State: to speak up in administrative bodies, or to address political assemblies or religious gatherings. In short, he had to be, in the words of Cato the Elder, *'vir bonus dicendi peritus'*, a good man and an able speaker.

A good lecture series was one that was well-organised, covered a reasonable amount of material, and was of a fixed length. First, the professor had to make sure that students were properly supplied with appropriate texts. If too little material existed, for instance, in the case of grammars or practice texts of Oriental languages, he had to compile them himself. Students were expected to have the book that the professor was using in front of them. Sometimes an author had to be omitted from the syllabus because there were too few copies of a particular text. How a book was dealt with depended on the students' intellectual prowess. A lecture might be merely introductory, explaining words and concepts, or paraphrases and translations would sometimes be used to penetrate to the general import of a text or its moral implications.

Some professors liked to dictate their lectures, but the governors tried to discourage this practice, preferring them to teach 'from memory'. Students were expected to take notes and were even advised to equip themselves with

▲ *Daniel Heinsius (1580-1655). Professor of Greek and history (1603-1655) and librarian (1607-1653)*

different kinds of notebooks, alphabetical tables or systematic collections of precepts and sayings. They were encouraged to think about what they had heard, and to write their notes out in full in their own rooms. 'A student who attends lectures every day but who does not recapitulate what he has learnt and make his own notes on it will derive little or no benefit,' warned Cocceius. 'As we see in church congregations', he added.

Ideally, a course would start by dealing with general principles and gradually move towards specific examples. First came theory, after which practical matters were addressed, beginning with what was known as *certum* or accepted fact and followed by the *controversum*, that is, matters that were as yet unresolved. Considerable time and attention were devoted to training the memory. And specificity was at a premium. Much prized was the ability to produce concrete examples or specimens.

Introductory courses were almost always conservative in nature. Philosophy had its own canon, with an Aristotelian framework into which new inventions in the sphere of natural history or cosmography were inserted. The medical faculty adhered to Galenus as interpreted by Fernel, the law faculty offered a very traditional treatment of Justinian's *Institutions*, and the theology faculty lectured on Church doctrine. However, in more advanced classes – in physiology and anatomy, in the treatment of the *Digest* and in polemics with non-Calvinist authors – students were introduced to more diverse opinions and more modern methods.

The full breadth of the eclectic principles that permeated Leiden's teaching became clear in disputations. These were seen, especially when they took the form of a seminar or *Collegium* (in which a small number of students would study a particular theme or book under a professor's guidance), as indispensable didactic instruments. 'The lectures are as sermons, the seminars as catechism,' wrote Gronovius. Opinions of every shade and angle could be aired at these seminars, including the latest, most advanced and boldest ideas.

Disputations were about gaining practice, not just in public speaking, but also in taking action and treating patients, applying the law in practice, or edifying a congregation. They primarily addressed subjects with some practical content: for medical students that meant pharmacology, therapeutic methods, and the systematic treatment of certain diseases; for law students it meant matrimonial and other contracts, wills, usufruct and oaths; for theologians it meant so-called *controversiae*, doctrinal issues and controversial points of view.

Balanced though the curriculum may have been, it was nonetheless prone to fundamental review, especially in response to changes in the prior education of incoming undergraduates. At the heart of these changes was the gradual emancipation of the humanities or 'philosophy', along with an ever greater diversity in the reasons for studying.

The Emancipation of the Humanities

The curriculum taught at Leiden University must be viewed in the context of Holland's idiosyncratic school system. At the end of the century, the United Provinces had what Jonathan Israel has described as 'a literacy-based culture developed to an extent which was wholly exceptional in Europe and which did not become normative elsewhere until centuries later'. Far-reaching urbanisation combined with a lack of universities had encouraged the development of large city schools that attracted hundreds of pupils from all over the country.

These schools were greatly influenced by the didactic ideas of Modern Devotion and the moral concepts of humanism. Their curriculum covered the entire range of scholarly pursuits: religious instruction, inculcating a passive and active command of Latin with stylistic exercises, Greek and Hebrew, and a fair dose of mathematics, logic and cosmography. The school's division into classes and that of the curriculum into a hierarchy of subjects – combined with a focus on eloquence and etiquette derived from classical texts – gave these schools a character of their own and made them into the gateway *par excellence* to the emerging cultural elite.

Immediately after the revolt against Spanish domination, these 'Latin schools', as they were known, evolved further into the ideal preparation for university. When the city of Alkmaar founded a new school in 1584, it defined

La Nouvelle Bibliotheque publique. 11

▲ *Interior of the library, 1712*

its objective as 'to cultivate the knowledge required for Leiden University in pursuit of the edification of the Church and the Conservation of the State.' Even the headmaster of a one-room school in Rhenen had to promise 'to ensure that his pupils were properly prepared for the university.'

The initial plans for a curriculum at Leiden University – proposals submitted by foreign professors who were unfamiliar with the Dutch situation – outlined a comprehensive, fourteen-year course of studies starting at the age of seven, patently inspired by the mediaeval curriculum of the university in Paris. The first seven years (*schola puerilis*) were taken up with lessons in Latin, Greek and Hebrew. These were followed by a *professorum collegium* for more advanced studies.

For those who were familiar with the situation in the United Provinces, the plans must have seemed anachronistic. By then, almost every major city in Holland had its own *schola puerilis*. Leiden University did try to bring the city school within its walls, but the city council had no intention of relinquishing control over it. These schools had their own clientele. By around 1650, the Latin schools were teaching about 14% of the relevant age group, far more than the 4% or 5% that attended the four universities in the United Provinces.

Leiden University did, however, help to determine the curricula of the Latin schools in the province of Holland. Its professors were involved in the drafting of the 1625 *Schoolordre* and produced their own textbooks, seeking to influence both the structure and the standard of education. The *Schoolordre* was a well thought-out and detailed plan that prescribed six classes and a strict timetable of days and times, subjects and authors, disputations and declamations, prizes and honours, all of which, of course, to be done in Latin. A series of new books saw the light: text editions and workbooks, grammars and dictionaries, the best known of which were Franco Burgersdijk's *Logica* and *Compendium* and Gerard Johannes Vossius's Latin grammar.

This involvement also gave Leiden's philosophy faculty a distinctive quality relative to similar faculties elsewhere. Initially, efforts were made – most notably under the influence of Justus Lipsius – to preserve the characteristics of the Parisian model. Apart from seeking to prescribe the order of the di-

◄ *Frontispiece to the* Catalogus Librorum *of 1716*

verse subjects, those involved also wanted to introduce public schools or colleges modelled on Oxford and Cambridge and similar colleges in France. They would serve as 'seminaries for superior men', selected from the youth of Holland and Zeeland and trained for positions of leadership in politics and the Church.

The resulting States College was consecrated in 1592, and although no others followed in its wake, this fairly small institution became the experimental garden for Leiden's philosophy education. This education was languishing. Good teachers were hard to find, but it is quite probable that the board of governors neglected their task here, because the Latin schools taught to such a high standard. For Lipsius, however, the purpose of a university was to inculcate *prudentia* and *sapientia*, prudence and wisdom, virtues that could be attained only through philosophy.

The problem that exercised minds the most was the level at which philosophy should be taught. From the outset, the faculty admitted students of different ages and different educational backgrounds. Not all Latin schools were equally good, besides which about half of the students were foreign. This diversity called for adjustments to the curriculum. At the outset, philosophy in Leiden reflected the educational standard of the Latin schools, and sought to instil a deeper understanding of the original classical texts. But for many students, this made the lectures too hard to follow, and it was this that led to a split in the programme: in their public lectures, the professors taught the official programme, and in private tutorials they discussed the material in more depth, in a compendium of their own making.

The success of this method, which was also adopted in other faculties, and which guaranteed a reasonably high standard of education in subjects that were regarded as both academically necessary and socially relevant, helped to alter the traditional hierarchy of disciplines. That is visible not only from the different way in which lectures were announced, but also from the salaries paid to the professors of different faculties. Initially, theologians and jurists earned considerably more than physicians and philosophers. But by around 1600, the gap had virtually closed. At the outset, philosophy served the same function as at a mediaeval university – it was a staging-post to the

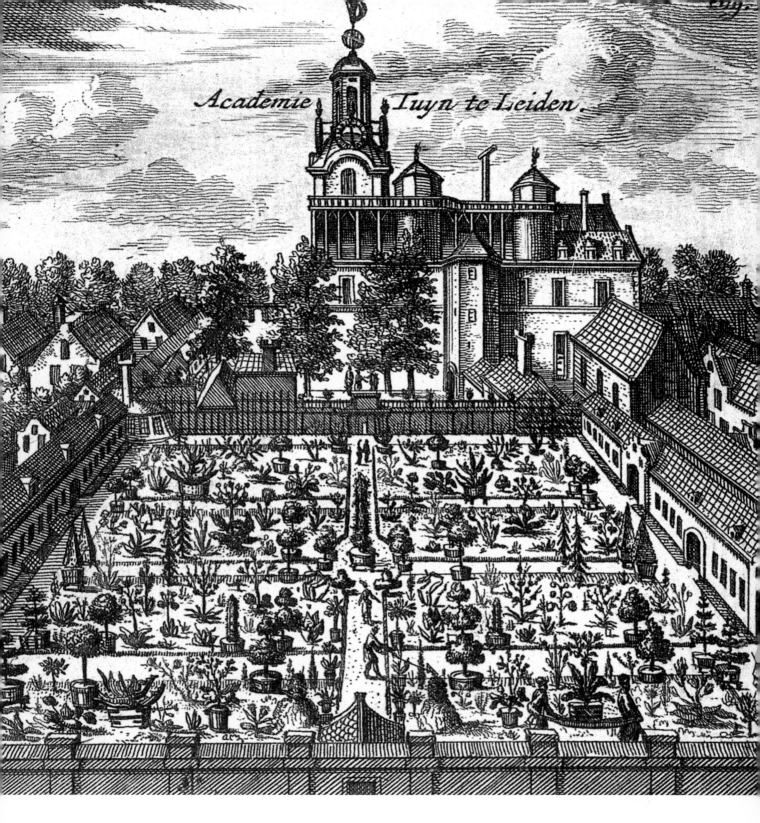

▲ *Botanical Gardens and rear of the main university building with observatory, 1712*

higher faculties. But this too changed in the latter half of the seventeenth century.

Although the division that was effected between philological studies and natural sciences was initially wholly artificial, it was the former that achieved its 'emancipation' first. The prominent philologists hired by the university bolstered the humanities' prestige. But natural philosophy also sought to enhance its status by borrowing from philology such rhetorical aids as emphasising its classical heritage or the moral import of its subjects. Another rhetorical 'argument' that philologists used to improve the status of their subject was the use of funerary monuments. A recent study shows that prior to 1630, it was almost exclusively professors in the humanities who had such monuments erected for themselves in St Peter's Church. It has been suggested that they did so mainly as a bid to boost their status and attract their colleagues' attention.

The process of differentiation eventually led to a parting of the ways. In the new statutes of the university, which were adopted in 1631, the original 'philosophy' faculty was renamed 'Faculty of Philosophy and the Good Arts'. Furthermore, these statutes no longer distinguished between the costs or weight attached to a doctorate from this faculty and those awarded by the others.

The emancipation of this faculty can also be inferred from the average age at which its students enrolled. At the beginning of the seventeenth century, the average new philosophy undergraduate was seventeen years of age, by 1700 he was over twenty, and by around 1775 he was 24. For purposes of comparison: the comparable figures for new law undergraduates were over 20, 22, and 20 years of age, and those for new medical undergraduates almost 22, over 23, and 23.

The Aims of University Study

In its first hundred years, Leiden University welcomed a total of some 26,000 students. Within fifty years after its foundation, it was already attracting an

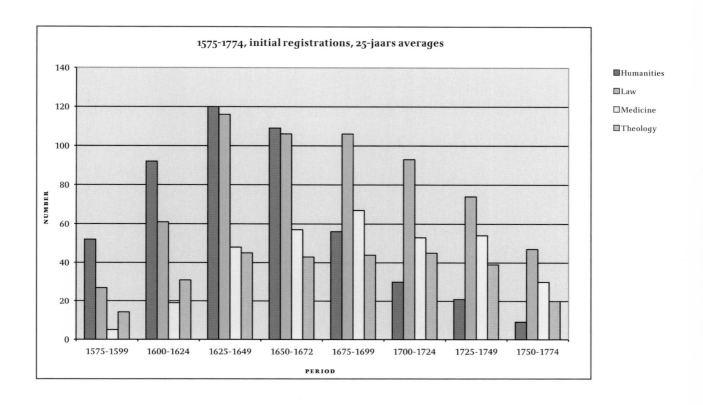

average of almost 400 students a year, over half of whom came from abroad. In its second century, the total number of students enrolled fell quite appreciably, to some 21,000, with a proportional decline in the number of foreign students.

The choice of faculty reveals a clear pattern. Interest in theology remained more or less constant at roughly 15 to 20 per cent, while law increased from 30 to 40 per cent. There were more drastic shifts in philosophy, from over 50 per cent to under 10 per cent of students, and in medicine, which rose from less than 10 per cent to almost a third of the total student population.

The picture becomes sharper once the figures for doctorates are taken into account. In the early years, few students were interested in taking a doctorate (the only degree awarded in this era). In the university's first 25 years, no more than six per cent of registered students (151 in total) gained a doctor's title. This proportion declined further to four per cent (241 out of a total of

► *The main university building in 1763*

5,607) over the following 25 years, before rising to eight per cent (748 out of 9,393) between 1625 and 1649, and subsequently to 16 per cent (1,270 out of 7,738) between 1650 and 1774.

The majority of doctorates (70 per cent or more) were awarded to students from the Netherlands. Law was by far the most popular subject. In the first quarter of the seventeenth century, 70 per cent of students awarded a doctorate had studied law, and even during the rest of the century, over 50 per cent came from the law faculty. Over 40 per cent were in medicine, while of the rest, about 3 per cent studied philosophy and about 2 per cent theology.

In the university's second hundred years, the doctor's title became more important. Compared to the 5 per cent of students who secured it at the beginning of the seventeenth century, by the third quarter of the eighteenth century this figure had risen to 44 per cent. Almost all of those concerned studied either law or medicine. But the trends in these two faculties were not identical. While the increase in the proportion of doctorates among medical students was enormous, from 20 per cent at the beginning of the seventeenth century to almost 60 per cent fifty years later, the corresponding increase among law students was truly spectacular: from 8 to 84 per cent!

If we compare the university's first and second hundred years, we are struck by a radical change in the purpose of studying. In the first hundred years, students did not choose a course with a view toward preparing for a specific profession. Although university education included practical training as well as theoretical orientation, very few students stayed on for the entire course of study. One must not forget, of course, that some students, Dutch as well as foreigners, were awarded doctorates from other, more prestigious universities, such as that of Orléans or Bologna. But this left many students who never gained one at all; they were less interested in professional training than in undergoing a kind of initiation into a cultural elite, a form of socialisation that placed more emphasis on formal discipline than on acquiring specific skills and knowledge.

In the university's second century, a stronger relationship developed between university studies and professional training. In the eighteenth century, Leiden's student population was divided more emphatically into two categories: burgher students preparing for a specific profession, and those from patrician or aristocratic backgrounds who were preparing to occupy a particular position in society. For the first group, studying was the most important activity at the university, and securing a doctorate was the primary aim. Those who belonged to the second group were quite content merely to attend university and participate in its social life.

The vast majority of Leiden's student population, two-thirds or more, originated from the upper middle classes. But in the first hundred years, there were also many students from lower social classes, including the sons of cobblers, carpenters, plumbers, house-painters, gardeners and cloth workers. For the contingent from Leiden or neighbouring cities such as The Hague, this proportion sometimes rose to as high as 25 per cent. In the second century, however, the proportion of students from the lower middle classes fell to 10 per cent.

A parallel trend can be traced among students from the social elite. In both centuries, there was a small but influential group of students from an aristocratic background. Some of them came from the highest echelons of society: princes of Bohemia and Brandenburg or the Polish prince Janus Radzivill, who enrolled on 14 April 1613, along with his high steward, his steward, his tutor and twelve of his aristocratic friends. Dutch royals and nobles, scions of the leading families of Zeeland, Friesland, Utrecht and Gelderland, and even members of the House of Orange, also came to study in Leiden. In total, 930 young noblemen enrolled in the first century, a little over three per cent of total student numbers.

We can gain a good indication of this aristocratic presence by looking at the 316 retainers or *famuli* who accompanied their noble masters to Leiden. In the second century, their numbers grew from 316 to 616, while the number of noblemen studying at the university actually declined, from 930 to 730. The explanation for this discrepancy lies in the proportion of high-ranking nobles. In the first century, Leiden welcomed 756 students from the lower and 174 from the higher nobility; in the second century these figures declined to 300 and 430, respectively. Leiden University clearly became more fashionable during the eighteenth century.

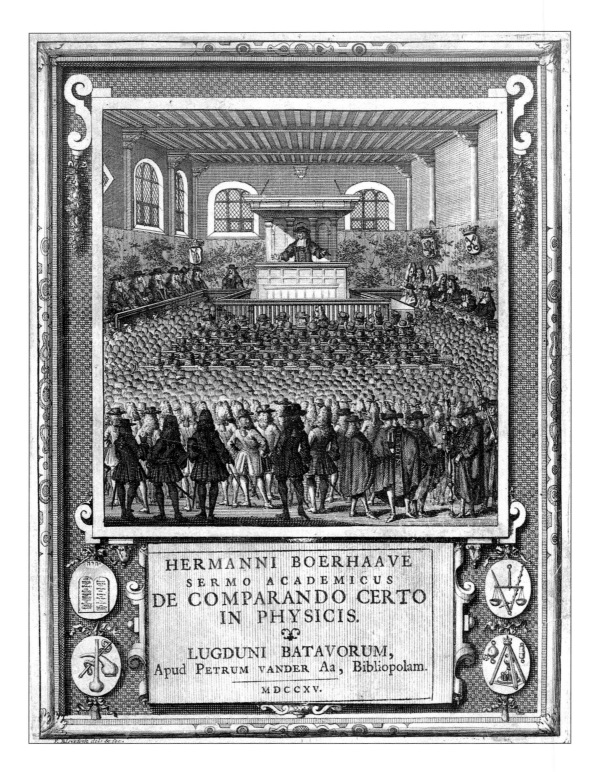

▲ *Title page of the inaugural address delivered by Herman Boerhaave (1668-1738),*
De comparando certo in physicis, *1715*

In general, we can say that the student population was a socially diverse body of young men with widely different reasons for studying. That tells us a great deal not only about the university itself, but also, and more notably perhaps, about the way it was viewed by the outside world. For the university itself, however, what mattered most was its success in welding the different groups with their divergent plans and goals into one whole. Unlike its students, the university pursued only one goal in the education it provided. In the eighteenth century, no less than in the previous period, this goal was to inculcate discipline.

Student Life

There was no absolute distinction, of course, between professional training and general academic development. Some students combined the two and studied diligently without neglecting the social side of student life. Most associated mainly with fellow countrymen, regardless of social origin. Foreign students frequently travelled to Leiden and enrolled together, and often rented rooms in the same house. British, French and German students all had their own houses or inns.

Some of these inns were actually run by compatriots, as in the case of the Yarmouth Arms, whose proprietor was Peter Powell. It was here that John Evelyn rented rooms in 1641, as did John Berry, eight years later, along with fourteen fellow-Englishmen. Friedrich Luca, who arrived in Leiden in 1665, immediately went to visit 'a great many compatriots ... who bade me a hearty welcome'. He rented rooms in the home of another German, 'and thus renewed that old Silesian acquaintance'. Dutch students from outside the province of Holland were also notorious for flocking together.

It was not just a question of bolstering their sense of security and making it easier to receive messages from home; students were also what we would now call ardent networkers. 'We pass'd our time in general very agreeably,' writes Alexander Carlyle, who stayed in Leiden for only a few weeks, 'and very profitable too, for ten to twelve of us held meetings at our lodgings, thrice a week in the evenings, when the conversation of young men of good knowledge, intended for different professions, could not fail to be instructive. Much more so than the lectures, which except two, that of civil law, and that of chemistry, were very dull.' Carlyle, who had gained his doctorate in Edinburgh, had plainly not come to Leiden for the benefits of attending lectures. As the son of a Calvinist minister, Carlyle was of humble origins, and his study trip abroad had been funded by a wealthy friend. His purpose in coming to Leiden was to expand his social network. When he arrived, in November 1745, he immediately noted in his diary that there were about 22 British students in Leiden. The list he drew up leaves us in little doubt as to the reason for his trip: he was hoping to meet some upper-class Englishmen.

All this socialising led to a certain standardisation in student life, which can be illustrated by looking at fashions in dress. From the late seventeenth century onwards, Leiden's students could be recognised by their Japanese-style chamber gowns. 'These students go to lectures and church wearing dressing gowns,' wrote the German traveller Heinrich Ludolph Benthem, 'and do not put on any respectable clothes for years on end.' A few years later, the casual attire also struck his fellow countryman Albrecht von Haller: 'People live in complete freedom here and go about the streets unrebuked in dressing-gowns.'

The uniformity of this curious outfit also mystified visitors. 'In those loose gowns,' Knapton confided to his diary, 'with sword, perukes, hats, brown slippers, and a book or two under their arms, they make an odd grotesque figure enough in the eyes of strangers.' Baron von Poellnitz even wondered if the city were not afflicted by some infectious disease: 'It made me think, the first time I passed through this town, that it had fallen prey to some epidemic. Indeed, all these dressing-gowns had an air of convalescence.'

Such trends towards conformity – from gowns and periwigs to initiation rituals and visits to inns and theatres – were actually encouraged, if indirectly, by the university. Leiden did not opt for the residential college system, in which students' progress was monitored at close quarters. It founded only one college, for Dutch theology students. This 'States College', which was housed in a former monastery, accommodated thirty to forty students. At its height in the early seventeenth century, with Festus Hommius at the helm, the College had about sixty students. They were fully trained as Protestant ministers there, studying first philosophy and then theology. The States of Holland bore the costs, and every major city in Holland and Zeeland was enti-tled to have two boys studying there at any one time (smaller towns could send one), boys who were frequently, though not always, from humble back-grounds. Its combination of philosophy and theology earned the College a reputation as 'Kuyle Josephs' (Joseph's pit), in which the great debates about Arminianism and Cartesianism were fought out in bitter earnest.

There were other forms of supervision. A 1581 census reveals that many students, who were registered separately, lived in a few large student houses. Most of these buildings were the property of private teachers, but one be-longed to the headmaster of the Latin school, Nicolaus Stochius, and another to a university professor, Rudolphus Snellius. The owners always had young schoolboys as well as students in their care. Stochius, for instance, accommo-dated 31 pupils and 20 students in his house, but Snellius's 21 'students' and the 16 living in Volcker Westerwolt's house must also have included schoolboys. These large houses, together with a few smaller boarding-houses, took in a total of 92 students, 36 per cent of the student population. Another 43 per cent (108 students) lodged in private houses, 11 per cent lived with their parents, and 10 per cent lived independently.

In the seventeenth century, professors often took lodgers too. Bronchorst, for instance, who discusses the subject at length in his diary, appears to have been fairly representative in having three to six students living in his house, eating at his expense and benefiting from free tuition. Physical and intellec-tual nourishment were combined in the most literal sense, since mealtimes were used for going over the day's lectures and testing students on their com-prehension of them.

In the eighteenth century, professors no longer took in student lodgers. But another custom endured and indeed appears to have become more en-trenched. Each student chose a particular professor, or was advised to do so, who would supervise his well-being, double as confessor and mentor, and keep his parents informed about their son's progress. This was a natural ex-

▲ *Student, third quarter of the seventeenth century*

▲ *Scholar, third quarter of the seventeenth century*

tension of the humanist concept of *contubernium*, living with one's students (literally sharing the same tent), as propounded in Leiden by Justus Lipsius. Besides requiring professors to set an intellectual and moral example to their students, it also imposed on them the commitment to take a lifelong interest in their protégés' careers.

For all the violence and dissipation that was associated in the public mind with student life, disciplinary measures and moral exhortations, sometimes but not always originating directly from the professors, were an increasingly dominant force. The whole idea of the *Forum Privilegiatum*, the special student court, was imbued with notions of discipline and correction. A case might be resolved in a variety of ways, the most common of which was a settlement between the parties. True, the sanctions imposed on proven offenders were generally far from severe. But that is because the consequences of punishment were taken into account. It was thought preferable to deal with youthful 'indiscretions' mildly rather than harshly. One should avoid picking unripe fruit, since it was bound to be a little sour.

Stiff penalties were imposed only in cases of group violence. Since public conduct was associated with honour, public order disturbances were always punished severely, unless the culprits proved sufficiently contrite and offered to pay appropriate compensation. '*Condonanda vitia non flagitia sunt,*' ('mistakes are forgivable, dishonourable deeds are not') said Cunaeus to the rowdy students protesting the death sentence imposed on a retainer of the Polish prince Radzivill, who had killed a night watchman. This was the sole instance of the court imposing the death penalty. In general, remorse was thought far more important than punishment.

This also explains why the senate declared war on the *nationes*, the regional clubs that the students set up independently. These clubs were seen as an infringement of the senate's authority and the source of various forms of misconduct. The first ban on these organisations was issued in 1592. That the ban had to be repeated in 1600, 1606, 1627 and 1641 reflects both the senate's signal lack of progress in this area and its determination to succeed. In 1659, three student *nationes* suspended their mutual hostilities to present a united front in their negotiations with the senate. Their show of solidarity sealed their fate, since it induced the senate to link the ban to the oath that the students had sworn upon enrolment.

This approach appears to have had the desired effect. It led, in any case, to the disbandment of the 'nation' of students from the eastern provinces of Gelderland and Overijssel, who left their armorial to posterity. A glance at its content reveals that in their own societies, the students simply copied the university's own disciplinary regime. The statutes included a variety of measures to curb violence and emphasised codes of conduct that were designed to prevent excesses and preserve the internal hierarchy. If discipline had been at the heart of the senate's concerns in seeking to eradicate the *nationes*, it could have saved itself the trouble. In fact, however, its actions seem rather to hark back to mediaeval disputes about who wielded authority at a university: the students, as had been the case at Bologna, or the professors, the Parisian model.

This did not alter the fact that the university as a whole was convinced that studying involved not merely gaining a fund of knowledge but also acquiring discipline, in a physical as well as an intellectual sense. The long list of skills associated with university studies, from fencing and riding to singing and dancing, arose from a desire to inculcate the control of mind over body, good posture, and the ability to keep time. The university authorities encouraged sports such as pall-mall and *kolf* (early forms of croquet and golf, respectively) as salutary forms of exercise.

Other forms of recreation were intended to serve a moral purpose; common pastimes included attendance at church services of different denominations and watching the execution of convicted criminals. Executions actually disrupted teaching at times, compelling professors to cancel lectures. Even visits to the theatre – a highly divisive issue in the Calvinist community – were recommended by some as a wholesome moral influence, on the grounds that witty censure from the stage could achieve more than earnest admonitions from the pulpit.

All this served to counter-balance trends within university education. This education had unquestionably shifted away from its original general programme to a far more specific curriculum, reflecting the university's own

transformation from a social institution to an educational establishment that trained students for certain professions. But this did not altogether eradicate the university's original social orientation. Although university education shifted, broadly speaking, from a course in the humanities to a training for future lawyers and physicians, the emphasis on discipline and character building was undiminished. The fundamental idea of the university remained to produce an administrative and professional élite to take up their rightful positions in society.

In that sense, students' expectations were no different from those of society at large. Whatever sources we consult, from manuals for the education of young nobles to models for raising future burghers, whether we look in 'mirrors' for princes or endure the gaze of the middle-class 'Spectators' [Dutch periodicals modelled on Addison and Steele's *Spectator*—transl.], the accent is always on general knowledge: too much specific knowledge was frowned upon, for king and subjects alike. Nero's disastrous rule was blamed on his intemperate passion for music. An ideal general education, argued the ancient Greeks and many seventeenth- and eighteenth-century thinkers, included 'learning to play the flute, but not too well.'

And just as a prince must strike a balance between knowledge and power, *Arte et Marte*, the Dutch merchant class must learn to combine wealth with wisdom, the commercial spirit with the study of philosophy. When Barlaeus addressed Amsterdam's city council at the opening of the city's college or 'Athenaeum Illustre' in 1632, and referred to the *mercator sapiens*, his words were wholly in line with the 'Spectatorial' periodicals published a hundred years later, which advised students to steer a middle course between debauchery and pedantry, between neglecting their studies and over-zealousness, between 'too much and too little worldliness'.

The Culture of Academia

Between too much and too little worldliness, between its international position and its local connections in Leiden, the university also cultivated region-

◄ *Student in gala costume, early eighteenth century*

al ties. It was a source of inspiration for a characteristic academic culture that spread from the province of Holland to the rest of the Netherlands. This can best be illustrated by looking at the four university institutes, all of which date from the end of the sixteenth century, and which were intended to form a single symbolic entity: the library, the anatomy theatre, the botanical gardens, and the fencing school.

The university library was not just an aid to study, it was the first public library in the Netherlands. It served as a meeting place for the learned and a centre for the wider community of scholars, printers and booksellers, who went there to exchange views as well as books. The library offered scholars not only peace and quiet, but also a substantial scholarly apparatus for studies of philology. In that sense, it was a general rather than a specialist library, which contained interesting objects besides books. It housed maps and globes, and portraits of scholars and famous men from the Republic of Letters.

By the mid-eighteenth century, this library had grown to a respectable 25,000 volumes and was emphatically designed to serve 'the public good'. Predicated on the assumption of scholarly use, it laid a clear emphasis on the classics, theology, and history, and was therefore not so very different from large private libraries. The long-term borrowing of books was very common, not only from public libraries but also from private individuals and even bookshops. The university library had two major shortcomings, however: what was produced in Leiden itself was not purchased so readily, and the burden of acquiring contemporary works in general was shifted to the professors themselves. The underlying assumption was that Leiden itself, including its booksellers and its printers, functioned as one vast library.

The anatomy theatre was the scene of dissections in the winter, when temperatures fell below freezing point. These were spectacular events for which lectures would be suspended; tickets were sold, and the entire senate would attend. Candles would be lit and the floor would be spread with fragrant herbs. The space could accommodate an audience of over three hundred, and during these theatrical demonstrations it would be filled to capacity. In the summer months, the theatre was used to exhibit the entire collection of skel-

► *Student wearing a Japanese-style chamber gown, early eighteenth century*

etons and specimens, engravings and instruments. For a while, the theatre was transformed into a museum dedicated to the brevity of human existence and the vanity of human desire. The exhibition included guided tours and catalogues.

The botanical gardens were intended to show *naturalia* and *artificialia* in a meaningful context. The three realms of the natural world – stones, plants and animals – were combined with implements from different cultures. It was here that the marked unity of the four institutions was most visible, comparable to the four humours or temperaments. The fourfold division represented the symbolic unity of life and death, of words and things, of the natural and the artificial. That was also the aim of the fourth institution, the fencing school, at which the themes of life and death, culture and nature, violence and control, were repeated in brief compass.

The fencing school taught riding, shooting and the technique of banner-waving as well as fencing: in other words, it taught all the skills that were required by militiamen and that were defined as civic duties. Instruction was based on mathematical principles and used geometrical figures inscribed on the floor indicating the correct position and posture. The teachers included Ludolph van Ceulen, a teacher of mathematics who is famed for his calculation of the constant π to 20 (and later 35) decimal places, a feat that he ordered to be inscribed on his gravestone. In 1600, Van Ceulen was also asked to teach civil and military technology. This course ('Nederduytsche Methematique' or Dutch mathematics) was taught in Dutch, and its students received thorough instruction in the building of fortifications.

With these institutes, the university became not just the top of the educational pyramid, but also the centre of a network of institutions and activities that together sustained a culture of learning and civilisation, intellectual curiosity and edification. Thus, Leiden was not only an important city for the book trade – Albrecht von Haller wrote in his diary, 'Entire streets are full of booksellers, and there is a printing press on every street corner' – but also, with renowned publishers such as Plantijn, the Elzeviers, Maire, Van der Aa, and Luchtmans, the main centre for the production of scholarly books.

The true centre of the book trade, of course, was Amsterdam. In 1688 the

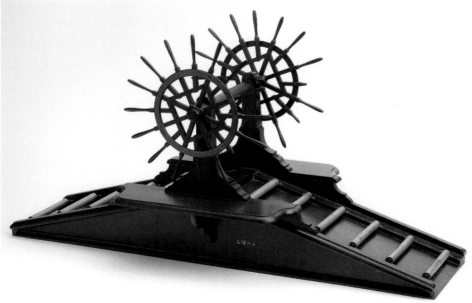

▲ *Model of a pneumatic pump, from the collection of the Theatrum Physicum ('physics theatre')*

▼ *Model of portage, from the collection of the Theater Physicum ('physics theatre')*

booksellers' guild in that city had no fewer than 186 members, extremely diverse and many of them highly specialised. But The Hague and Rotterdam too were flourishing centres of the book trade, and Haarlem, Gouda and Delft also boasted a rich tradition in this area. Not only these cities, but smaller towns too, such as Edam, Enkhuizen and Hoorn, had local libraries. Combined with the substantial book ownership among private individuals, at least among the well-to-do – the libraries of regents and wealthy burghers probably contained an average of 100 to 200 volumes – and the growing popularity of reading clubs in the eighteenth century, the Dutch propensity for reading was striking, especially when viewed in its international context.

Besides collecting books, many burghers were avid collectors of *naturalia* and artefacts, 'objects of *vertu*'. Here too, Leiden University provided the most important institutionalised example. Its collection of 'curiosities', which was on public show in the covered passage in the botanical gardens and the anatomy theatre's summer exhibition, attracted crowds of enthusiastic visitors from home and abroad. It contained human and animal skeletons, specimens and instruments, seeds and dried plants, exotic objects from all five continents and a large collection of prints.

All this was displayed in the service of scholarship. The collection was a pendant of the library. Collecting antiquities, like studying philology, was seen as a means of restoring classical antiquity. Like classical literature, the exhibits expressed the fullness of existence. But just as classical texts exerted a moral influence, the theatre's collection depicted the diversity of God's dealings with Man. Its *pièce de résistance* consisted of two skeletons (one with a spade, the other with an apple) separated by a tree around which coiled a serpent. In other words, the scene represented Paradise with Adam and Eve, but not as a garden and a symbol of life, but quite the opposite, as an *anatomie moralisée* symbolising mortality and death.

In other cities too, collections of this kind were sometimes combined with botanical gardens or anatomy theatres. But they were not confined to such settings. Collecting curiosities was an activity pursued with fervour and no mean financial investment by a large proportion of the burgher population. They were enabled to do so by large flows of trade that linked the province to the entire world, so that this leisure pursuit was largely reserved for affluent townspeople in cities with offices of the trading companies: most notably Amsterdam, but also Hoorn and Enkhuizen, Delft and Rotterdam.

These collections acquired a different quality in the course of the eighteenth century. While initially encyclopaedic in nature, presenting miniature versions of 'the world at large', they gradually became more specialised, for instance focusing only on *naturalia*, or even perhaps only on shells. But the number of collectors continued to grow, aided by a substantial bulk trade and by specialist shops, lending an exotic air to the interior of many of Holland's burgher homes and giving some foreign visitors the impression that Holland itself was an outlandish place.

Besides – and as an extension of – this passion for collecting, Holland had a thriving garden culture, and in this respect too, the university was in the province's vanguard. Its botanical gardens were initially intended 'to promote the study of medicinal herbs'. Still, what developed was not so much a *hortus medicus* as a *hortus botanicus*, in which only one-third of the plants had medicinal properties and many were of far-flung provenance. Eager to obtain new specimens, the garden's first superintendents maintained regular contact with the trading companies, and built special glasshouses in which to keep non-hardy plants in the winter, using a stove to keep them alive.

Leiden's botanical gardens were not unique, but they did create a certain accent amid a network of multifarious gardens. As time went by, other cities acquired their own botanical gardens, the largest being the one that opened in Amsterdam in 1682. What is more, a multitude of nurseries mushroomed in the sandy soil behind the dunes near Leiden, Haarlem and Alkmaar. The work that went on there, and in private gardens ranging from the small herb and kitchen gardens, orchards and allotments with sheds in the outskirts of every city to large country estates such as Buitensorgh, Hofwijck and Sorgvliet, was a collective activity in which scientific, economic and social motifs were seamlessly interlaced.

In its anatomy theatre, too, the university played a pioneering role in the United Provinces. Besides being used for anatomy lessons, the theatre was also the scene of experimental physiology research; vivisection (mainly using

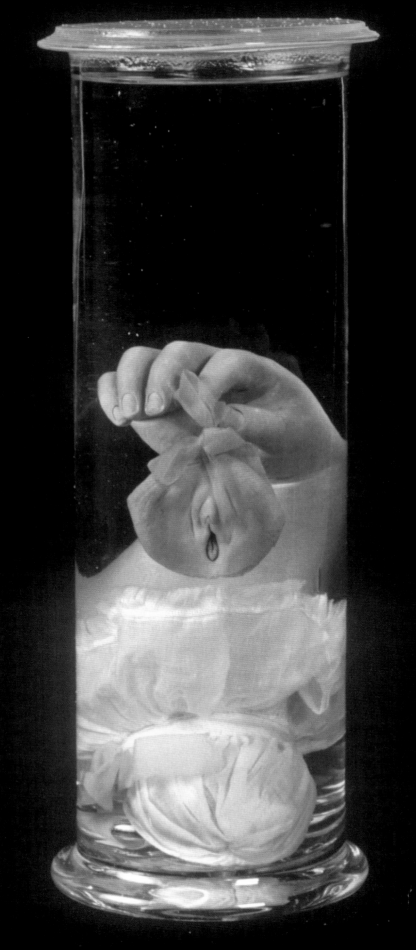

dogs) became a popular means of researching circulation and the functions of the glands and reproductive organs in the seventeenth century. There were many other anatomy theatres around the country. The surgeons' guilds of Amsterdam and Delft, The Hague and Dordrecht, Rotterdam, Alkmaar and Haarlem all had their own dissecting rooms. Those of Leiden and Amsterdam, Delft and The Hague, in particular, developed into more than venues for surgery lessons. In conjunction with the library, the collection of curiosities and the botanical gardens, these theatres grew into veritable cultural centres, where scientific research, artistic production and economic activity went hand in hand, and where popular entertainment blended naturally with social stratification.

Finally, the university also played a pioneering role in the dissemination of technological expertise. The military and civil technology course, launched in 1600 at the behest of Prince Maurits himself and devised by Simon Stevin, taught an enormously diverse group of burgher students and craftsmen the theory and practice of diverse skills such as the building of fortifications, surveying, and navigation. In the eighteenth century, this technological expertise, as disseminated by the university, was incorporated into regular classes in mathematics and astronomy, chemistry and natural history. To this end, the university set up diverse physics and chemistry laboratories, where leading popularisers of Newtonian science such as Boerhaave, 's-Gravesande and Musschenbroek combined experimental philosophy with advanced work in steam and electricity.

The university did not confine itself to these activities. A university city was also pre-eminently, as we have seen, a place that attracted a motley crowd of private teachers seeking to advance the students' 'noble and virtuous education'. Holland's other major cities, too, became arenas for small 'knowledge entrepreneurs', many of whom focused on cognitive or scientific fields such as arithmetic, linguistics, mathematics, physics, chemistry and astronomy. Even lessons in farming or mercantile skills were taught by such itinerant purveyors of knowledge, in styles ranging from the semi-scholarly to the downright colloquial.

Another boon, of at least equal significance, was that eminent professors

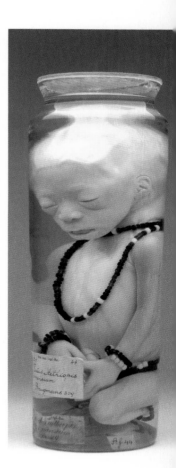

◄ *Preparation, probably made by Frederik Ruysch (1638-1731)*
► *Human foetus from the Brugmans collection*

and lowly entrepreneurs alike produced textbooks and manuals that enabled many people not attached to any seat of learning to expand their knowledge through independent study. Initially these were mainly books about surveying and navigation, and popular legal or medical knowledge – lexicons for notaries, new techniques for surgeons – but other subjects were gradually added, such as agriculture and horticulture, livestock farming and natural history, experimental physics and chemistry, hydraulic engineering and mill building.

All this meant that there was no decline in intellectual standards. In many respects, Leiden University seems to have been immune to the general decline that manifested itself throughout the Dutch Republic at this time. Even in 1765, the famous *Encyclopédie* published by Diderot and D'Alembert was still referring to it as 'the leading [university] in Europe'. It seemed clear, ob-

▲ *Design for the placing of the Papenbroek marbles in the Orangerie*

served these Enlightenment spokesmen, that all of the great names from the Republic of Letters went there to contribute to its glory. In classical and Oriental philology, history and Roman law, theology and philosophy, natural science and medicine, the teaching was invariably of a high standard, in some cases, extremely high, throughout the eighteenth century. Nor was there any decline in interest in administrative skills or technology – in other words, for the practical side of the university curriculum; on the contrary, these subjects attracted an ever keener interest in the eighteenth century.

The one problem was that education had become too compartmentalised; the various parts of the educational pyramid had become overly specialised. As a result, supply and demand were out of alignment. The demand was for courses with a more practical orientation, for skills that were less specifically academic but more fruitful commercially. The more 'modern' elements of higher education, as expressed in classes dealing with ways of controlling nature and applications of political science, were therefore not disseminated widely enough in society, and remained confined to the classical culture of scholarship, of which the university remained the bastion.

The Marriage of Mars and the Muses

The four engravings that the Leiden printer Andreas Cloucq published in 1610, depicting the four institutions that the university had established at the end of the sixteenth century, were consciously intended to evoke the popular university pun on the theme of *Arte et Marte*. Cloucq and the engraver, Willem Swanenburgh, based their prints on drawings by Jan Cornelis van 't Woud. The university library, the anatomy theatre, the botanical gardens and the fencing school were all depicted with immense attention to detail and with visible pride.

The importance of these engravings and their influence on the university's self-image can scarcely be overstated. They were frequently copied and reproduced in books, either reduced in size or folded and incorporated into the binding. Important books such as Orlers' history of Leiden and Meursius's

Athenae Batavae, which were crucial in determining the image of Leiden University at home and abroad, showed that the university not only had great scholars within its walls, but that it also possessed institutions attesting to a great creative spirit.

In his address at the beginning of lectures in June 1575, the theologian Ludovicus Capellus described the new university as a place 'where peaceful studies would be combined with the deeds of war'. Anyone who professed astonishment at this combination, he went on, had evidently forgotten that Pallas in a suit of armour was the same goddess who appears at other times in 'civilian' dress, the vigilant leader in both combat and learning.

Capellus's colleagues in the senate recognised this duality, as is clear from the coat of arms that they chose for the university. The initial proposal, submitted on 20 July 1576, was for an image of armed Pallas wielding a shield. On her shield would be blazoned the arms of Holland and the House of Orange above those of Zeeland and Leiden. The design that was eventually approved showed Pallas in a niche, surrounded by the arms of the House of Orange, Holland and Leiden.

There is no documentation explaining why Zeeland's arms fell by the wayside, but the significance of the other three coats of arms is obvious. The university's task of service was its *raison d'être*. The final version of the coat of arms also alludes to the goddess's two talents, as recalled by Capellus, for the university's Seal depicts Pallas engrossed in an open book. She is still in a coat of mail, with cuirass and helmet, and her left hand still rests on the terrible Gorgon shield. Yet at the same time, she is absorbed in her studies: her attitude is aggressive and meditative at the same time.

Dousa must have recognised this same duality within himself. He was a nobleman of Holland, lord of Noordwijk. He had studied in Leuven, Douai and Paris. An accomplished neo-Latin poet, he had also played a crucial role in organising the resistance to the siege of Leiden by the Spanish troops in 1574. That is exactly how Cornelis Visscher depicts him, as a learned warrior, clad in a cuirass but with his hand on a book bearing his personal motto: 'Sweet above all are the Muses'. A verse caption beneath the print, by Petrus Scriverius, states: 'The valiant lord of Noordwijk had not only the glorious Muses

CHRISTOPHORVS PLANTINVS
ANNO· 158 ₄ · ÆTATIS· 6 ₄·

on his side, but he also possessed all the qualities of the god of war.'

  This was also the picture that had been formed in the public mind of the university's founder, William of Orange. Bonaventura Vulcanius, the university's first true Greek scholar, noted in an address given in 1591-92 that William, 'whom we may rightly call *Mars togata*, the learned god of war' had created the university in the wisdom of his foresight as a bastion against the coarsening influence of war on Holland's youth, 'that his land of Batavia

▲ *Christophe Plantijn (1514-1589), university printer (1583-1585)*

might be rich not only in the strength that would protect the Fatherland by acts of war, but also in the good counsel and wisdom needed to preserve it.'

This combination continued to serve as a guiding *topos*, as is clear from its role in the celebration of the university's 50th and 150th anniversary celebrations (the 100th, in 1675, was not celebrated because of the political tumult in the period leading up to it). In 1624, Petrus Cunaeus posed the question: why had the university flourished so well in its first 35-year period and yet faltered during the twelve-year truce with Spain, from 1609 to 1621? During this truce, the university had been paralysed by the acrimonious dispute between the Arminians and Gomarists, which ended with the National Synod at Dordrecht and the reduction of the university to a Calvinist institution. Cunaeus answered his own question by invoking the twin gifts of Pallas, in whom prowess in words and martial deeds went together. He told his audience that if this Pallas lived anywhere, it must surely be among the people of Holland.

Franciscus Fabricius, speaking as rector of the university in 1725, exploited the rhetorical potential of this *topos* to its fullest extent in his *Oratio in natalem tertium Academiae Lugduno Batava*. He described Janus Dousa as one 'surpassed by no one in the skills of war and learning (which only when conjoined can make a true, immortal Nobility).' And he continued in the same vein. Were laws silenced by war? Had not Jan van Brabant founded Leuven after a war had ended? Maybe so. But Leiden University had been founded 'amid one of the deadliest wars of all', and it was a fact 'that Pallas herself bore arms at that time, and that the burghers of this city, their weapons glinting and rifles blazing, led the new Professors through the public thoroughfares to the university.'

◄ *Procession for PhD award ceremony in front of the main university building, c. 1650*

HERMANN. BOERHAAVE. VOORHOUT. BATAV

BOTANICES ET MEDICINAE PROFESS. OBDIN. $\frac{20}{3}$ MDCCIX.
DEIN ET CHEMIAE, POSTEA. MEDICINAE PROF. ORD.
NATUS $\frac{31}{12}$ MDCLXVIII, OBIIT $\frac{23}{9}$ MDCCXXXVIII.

GUL. IAC.'s GRAVESANDE, SILVA-DUCENSIS.

MATHES. ET ASTRON. PROFESS. ORDIN. $\frac{22}{6}$ MDCCXVII, DEIN ET PHILOSOPHIAE.
NATUS $\frac{28}{9}$ MDCLXXXVIII, OBIIT $\frac{28}{2}$ MDCCXLII.

BERNARDUS SIEGFRIDUS ALBINUS, FRANCOFURT

MARCH. PROFESSOR ANATOMES & CHIRURGICAE
ORDINAR. $\frac{13}{10}$ MDCCXXI, DEIN & MEDICINAE $\frac{9}{8}$ MDCCXLV.
NATUS $\frac{24}{2}$ MDCXCVII. OBIIT $\frac{9}{9}$ MDCCLXX.

GERARDUS NOODT, NEOMAGO-GELRUS.

NEOMAGI, DEIN FRANEQ., POSTEA ULTRAI., TANDEM
LEIDÆ. IUR. PUBL. ET PRIV. PROF. ORD. $\frac{31}{8}$ MDCLXXXV.
NATUS $\frac{4}{3}$ MDCXLVII, OBIIT $\frac{15}{8}$ MDCCXXV.

2

Freedom and Restraint

LEIDEN
UNIVERSITY
1775-1975

Contract and compromise

The end of the *ancien régime* in the Netherlands was accompanied by a fanfare of unrest but no radical change. Like the old Republic, the new Kingdom was an equilibrium machine. The elite retained the power to protect their own interests at the same time as serving the public good. While conflicts of interests in the Republic had been resolved within a system of factions, the Kingdom accommodated religious and ideological differences through cooperation between the denominational and political 'pillars' that were to become such a distinctive feature of Dutch society. The 'contracts of correspondence' of the eighteenth century were now recast as forms of compromise.

In the meantime, the powerful Dutch Republic had shrunk to the Netherlands, a country that had little option but to accept the influence and at times interference of its larger neighbours. Even so, through its rapid modernisation and substantial colonial possessions, this small nation forged a special position for itself amid the great powers, a position it managed to sustain even when these possessions were lost after the Second World War. As a small trading nation, the Netherlands subscribed to a characteristic amalgam of self-interest and altruism. The dialectics of freedom and restraint that arose from this mindset are not only broadly typical of the country as a whole, but also placed their stamp on its universities, and on Leiden University in particular.

Freedom and Restraint

Although the contrast implicit in *arte et marte*, words versus arms, the contemplative versus the active life, has entirely different emotional overtones from the clash between 'freedom and restraint', in the Dutch setting the two were clearly related. This is expressed elegantly by Frans Hemsterhuis, a philosopher who operated at the fault line between Enlightenment and Romanticism. In one of his essays, he ponders, in reference to the Dutch Republic, the 'almost unparalleled phenomenon of a nation that was magnificent in wartime and contemptible to the point of absurdity in times of peace'.

Hemsterhuis's essay forges a link between the state of war and the power of central authority. In peacetime, there was a general inclination to reduce this authority's powers in favour of the law, a trend carried to such lengths that eventually nothing remained of that authority, and the law could no longer be upheld. The interplay between freedom and dependency that Hemsterhuis identified was a reformulation of the old contrast between *arte et marte*. The new Kingdom, which had to strike a compromise between monarchy and democracy, between constitution and freedom, would find itself embroiled in it. As would Leiden University.

The relationship between freedom and restraint is a *topos* with deep roots in classical antiquity and Dutch history. Far more dramatically than the opposition between *arte et marte*, it was the concept of freedom at moments of disaster that played a decisive role in the foundation of Leiden University. In William of Orange's letter of 28 December 1574 to the States of Holland, he urged the founding of a university 'as a pillar and buttress of the country's freedom and its sound and lawful national government'. He saw the university as the ideal instrument for preventing the country's enemies from continuing 'their rampant tyranny and oppression of both the country's religion and its freedom, by force or often by subterfuge'. The university would be 'the castle and fortress [*blochuys*] of the entire country'.

William's source for this description is unknown. On the one hand, his choice of the word *blochuys* has clear Biblical overtones – Psalm 18 contains the line 'The Lord is my rock, and my fortress', which in Philip van Marnix's

▶ *Students leaving the main university building after the address delivered by Professor Cleveringa on 26 November 1940*

BENJAMIN MARIUS TELDERS

Geboren 19 Maart 1903- buitengewoon hoog
leraar in het Volkenrecht te Leiden 1931 –
gewoon hoogleraar in het Volkenrecht en de
Inleiding tot de Rechtswetenschap 1937-
op 18 December 1940 door de Duitsers gear
resteerd wegens activiteit tegen het onrecht
door hen gepleegd - draagt zijn opsluiting
in de gevangenis te Scheveningen en de
concentratiekampen te Buchenwald, Vught,
Sachsenhausen en Bergen-Belsen in onge
broken geestkracht & is daar een steun voor
en redder van vele medegevangenen-sterft
in het vernietigingskamp Bergen-Belsen
op 6 April 1945

MILES PRAESIDII LIBERTATIS

Dutch translation is rendered *'God is mijn borcht, mijn blochuys sterc end' vast'*. On the other hand, in using the phrase 'buttress of the country's freedom and its sound and lawful national government' (*'tot onderhoudt der vryheyt ende goede wettelicke regieringe des lants'*), William may well have been thinking of Livy. There is a similar phrase in the first Dutch translation of Livy's *Ab urbe condita* (1541). Whatever the case may be, it is this passage in Livy that governed the next stage in the shaping of Leiden's myth of freedom.

This myth was a creation of the liberalism associated with Leiden. The motto *Libertatis praesidium*, which the university adopted in 1917 as the circumscription for its new seal — an oval version of the original sixteenth-century seal — derived from an address given in 1875 by the assistant rector, Matthias de Vries, as part of the university's centennial celebrations. He recalled, in Latin and in the presence of representatives of other universities, that William of Orange had wanted a university 'that would serve as a bastion of independence and civilisation.' In his foundation day speech the year before, De Vries (then rector) had described Leiden University as an institution 'that had always been the bastion of liberty'. The motto was included in Dutch in a pamphlet issued to accompany the student masquerade in June 1875, and in Latin in the caption to an allegorical print with a list of all the professors since 1575: 'Leiden University, monument of strength, glory of the land, bastion of liberty.'

Thus, ever since the 1875 centenary, *Libertatis praesidium* and its Dutch equivalent *'Bolwerk der vrijheid'* (bastion of liberty) had become a commonplace, and in 1917, the phrase was adopted as the university's motto. It should be noted that De Vries was not its author. He derived it from the classical scholar Petrus Hofman Peerlkamp, who had used these words in his rector's address in 1839, which De Vries had attended as a student. His patriotic heart swelled with pride upon hearing that his university had been founded, in Peerlkamp's words, 'in such circumstances, in such a city, at such a juncture, and with such expedition, that it seemed to have descended from the heavens by divine Providence as a bastion of independence.' Yet even Peerlkamp was not the initiator of this description. He borrowed it straight from Livy's *Ab Urbe condita*, which brings us back to where we started, with William of

◄ *Plaque of the Leiden lawyer, Professor B.M. Telders, in the small auditorium of the main university building*

▲ *Stained-glass window in the main auditorium, with Professor Telders in the centre*

▲ *Stained-glass window in the main auditorium: William of Orange, Hugo de Groot, Van Hogendorp,*
Dousa, Snouck Hurgronje, Thorbecke, Van Vollenhoven, Huizinga and Lorentz

Orange and the founding of Leiden University.

It is not entirely certain that Peerlkamp identified William of Orange's description of a university in his letter of 28 December 1574 with the phrase used by Livy. But that he was familiar with William's letter is beyond dispute. In his address he expatiated on the university's relations with the House of Orange, dwelling in particular on scions of that House who had studied there. Furthermore, there are unmistakeable similarities between the picture cherished by patriotic liberal scholars regarding William's noble intentions and the story related by Livy.

That story, from the third book, in which Livy discusses the dramatic conflict between the senate and the plebeian party in 305 BC, depicts an institutional crisis of a depth similar to that experienced by the Netherlands in 1574. The reforms it prompted served to protect the rights and the freedom of the people. Decisions taken by the people were declared binding for all, including the nobles. Another law created the possibility of an 'appeal to parliament, a bastion of liberty unique in its kind.'

The concept of liberty was thus used in a zigzagging analogy that linked the university's past to its recent history. What is more, the identity distilled from this motto was to acquire the value of a self-fulfilling prophecy many years later, at a time when that identity was tested and all liberty seemed irrevocably lost: following the German invasion of May 1940. While it is true that the university tried to maintain its regular routine during the first few months after the cease-fire between Dutch and German forces, the difficulty of doing so became clear in September when the departing rector Frederik Muller, a great Latin scholar but an arrogant man, gave his farewell address. With Seyss-Inquart's representative for South Holland in the audience, Muller wound up his speech with a glorification of the principle of leadership and the splendid prospect 'that our Dutch nation will finally become accustomed to discipline'. There must have been a painful silence in the large auditorium when he stopped speaking.

The next reaction from the university was very different. On 23 October the so-called Aryan declaration was distributed to all university staff. The senate planned to discuss the subject on 26 October in response to a strong protest drafted by the jurist B.M. Telders. The occupying forces prevented the meeting from going ahead, but views were exchanged anyway, in small groups of fewer than twenty (the number of people permitted to meet without special permission). It was eventually decided to sign, but to lodge individual protests. Seventeen hundred students signed a similar declaration of protest.

On 23 November, the German occupying forces proceeded to dismiss all 'non-Aryan' staff, as a result of which the law faculty lost two of its professors. It was decided to stage a protest during the next scheduled lecture that would normally be taught by one of these two, Professor E.M. Meijers. At 10 a.m. on Tuesday, 26 November, the dean of the faculty, Professor R.P. Cleveringa, made what was to become a famous speech. He read out the letter of dismissal

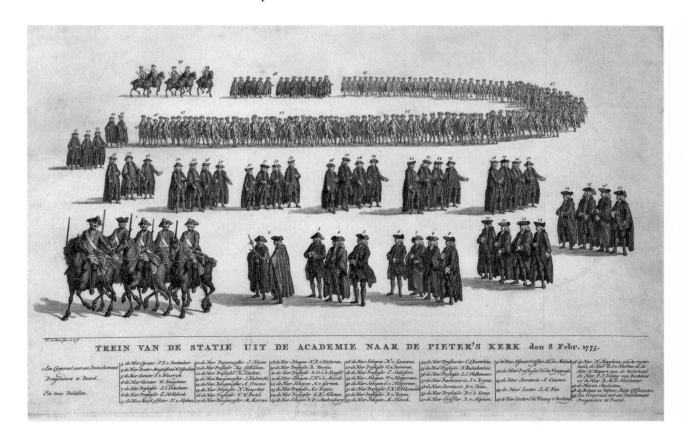

TREIN VAN DE STATIE UIT DE ACADEMIE NAAR DE PIETER'S KERK den 8 Febr. 1775.

▲ *Procession of professors, officials and students on their way from the main university building to St Peter's Church on 8 February 1775* 'in all its stark grossness' and without any discussion of the Germans' motives: 'Their deed merits no further comment'. He went on to discuss the significance of Professor Meijers, who had been his teacher:

> All I desire at present is to banish them [the German occupying forces] from our sight and to rise above them, and to direct your gaze to the height at which stands the inspiring figure of the man whose fate has brought us here today. For it seems to me right that we should try clearly to impress upon ourselves at this moment in time whom it is that this power, which enjoys no support outside itself, is casually sweeping aside after a working life of thirty years.

Cleveringa's speech was as measured as it was courageous. He deliberately refrained from making any political statement and did not discuss the racist principle underlying the dismissal. Indeed, the address was intended in part to forestall any rash student demonstrations. But the stark black-and-white juxtaposition made his speech highly effective. The following day, the students boycotted lectures in protest, and the occupying forces closed the university. The students had already expressed their opposition in the illegal periodical *De Geus*, first published on 4 October 1940. The anatomist Barge and the theologian Van Holk would use their lectures to expose the fallacies of the racist Nazi ideology.

More dismissals followed. Telders was arrested and sent to a concentration camp. He was to die in Bergen-Belsen on 6 April 1945. Meijers too ended up in a concentration camp, but survived the war. Cleveringa was detained for a total of 18 months, but was eventually released. In the meantime, the German forces tried to refashion the university to their liking, by tightening up the rules, dismissing some staff and appointing pro-German replacements. But following a few more dismissals – most crucially that of Roelof Kranenburg in March 1942, on the grounds that his book on administrative law paid scant attention to ordinances issued by the occupying forces – a large proportion of the teaching staff resigned of their own accord (including 53 out of 68 professors). Between October 1940 and August 1944, some 40 of

Leiden's lecturers would be imprisoned for varying periods of time. The result was the myth of a university that had proved itself worthy of its motto.

Legislation

Besides the political debate that filled the waning days of the *ancien régime*, the education system too attracted fundamental criticism. Here, however, pragmatic, gradual change prevailed over radical upheaval. Visionary plans were certainly launched for the renewal of the old fabric of education, especially during the 'Batavian Republic' (1795-1806) and the brief period of French rule (1806-1813). This debate produced in outline three paradigmatic alternatives. The first, generally seen as a 'French model', highlighted usefulness and practical applications: it envisaged a heavily centralised system and aimed at dismantling universities into faculty schools. The second model emphasised the representation of scholarship and is associated with the development of the German university. The idea here was to create a single 'super-university', while reducing all of the other institutions to preparatory schools or colleges preparing students for the professions in general and 'incubators' for professorships in particular. The third was predicated on a view of higher education as a general civilising force inculcating a broad general education, and envisaged the continuation of the existing wide-ranging field of higher education that had evolved in the Dutch Republic.

This third option, slightly admixed with elements of the other two, would eventually carry the day. French rule lasted only a few years, and the effect on higher education did not penetrate beyond the surface. There was certainly nothing utilitarian or centralistic about the spirit of the 1815 Education Act. The new legislation did not prioritise direct applications of learning; it was up to the faculty or the professor to determine matters of educational content. This content continued to be characterised by a wide-ranging foundation course and a cohesive curriculum informed by humanist principles, seeking to inculcate 'a clearly-defined and uniform system of skills': in the words of Johan Huizinga, 'practical and noble, neither profound nor adventurous'.

▲ *Postcard depicting the main university building, c. 1900*

Scarcely had the 1815 Education Act entered into effect when a growing chorus of disgruntled voices started calling for change. Yet it was to remain in force (barring a few modifications) for half a century, when it was superseded by the 1876 Higher Education Act. The new legislation breathed an entirely different ethos. The material taught in the foundation course was moved to the newly created classical grammar school or *gymnasium*. This, combined with the introduction of master's degrees for a range of clearly-defined specialist subjects, consigned the encyclopaedic nature of higher education and its humanist aims to the past.

From then on, university courses were designed as preparation for a profession, and students counted out a long rosary of examinations in supplication for a successful position in society. Sharp dividing lines criss-crossed the field of scholarship: each subject was distinct and narrowly defined. Anything not covered by these specialist disciplines was banished from the university. Higher education became an altogether more *schoolish*, pragmatic business, and the centrifugal forces to which universities were exposed soon unleashed a fresh chorus of criticism, partly fuelled by nostalgia for the old Education Act. All this emphasis on specialisation had entirely overshot the mark; such was the unceasing lament between the First and Second World Wars.

Yet this Act too proved difficult to supplant. Minor changes aside, it would endure until 1960, with the passage of the University Education Act. This Act was linked to the simultaneous radical overhaul of Dutch secondary schools effected by the Secondary Education Act (*Mammoetwet*). Until then, sectoral divisions along lines of theory and practice between schools of different levels had essentially perpetuated class distinctions; the new classifications allowed for more mobility and a range of hybrid forms in a system geared towards the personal development of each pupil and student.

Compared to the 1876 Act, the new legislation essentially reversed the hierarchy between theory and practice, knowledge and applications. The goal of education now became: 'to inculcate the ability to pursue independent studies, to prepare for the exercise of positions in society requiring academic training, and to foster insight into the relations between different branches

of learning.' Section 2 of the Act added a third objective: to instil 'a sense of
civic responsibility'. Essentially, the same objectives that had once been formulated in the 1815 Act thus made their return, albeit formulated in different
terms and in an entirely different context.

Management and Administration

In each of these successive pieces of higher education legislation, the contrast
between freedom and restraint was a recurrent theme. This is clearest from
the way in which university management was organised. Although the 1815
Act preserved the old board of governors, it did not leave the eighteenth-century status quo intact. Under the *ancien régime*, the university had been a
body with a legal personality, one that enjoyed substantial administrative and
financial independence as well as far-reaching privileges; post-1815, on the
other hand, the university was a state institution that possessed no independence under public law and did not occupy a special position in relation to other
institutions. While in previous centuries the board of governors had been
able to pursue its own financial policy, after 1815 a budget, approved by the
king, provided the guidelines for payments made by or on behalf of the ministry of the interior. Where the board of governors had initially been free to appoint professors as they saw fit, from now on professors were appointed by
the king – albeit on the basis of the board's nominations.

In other respects too, the board of governors' powers were curtailed. Even
so, their responsibilities remained substantial: ensuring compliance with all
legislation governing higher education, monitoring the quality of education,
caring for the university's buildings and its other property, appointing junior
staff, disbursing funds, and keeping proper financial records. Even after the
new Higher Education Act became law in 1876, the board of governors retained its administrative involvement in numerous activities, although its
role was now described explicitly as that of a 'mediating agency' between
ministry and university. Rather than being the university's representatives
in its dealings with the ministry, after 1876 the board of governors became

▲ *An address by the rector in St Peter's Church to mark the university's third centenary on 8 February 1875*

the ministry's representatives in its dealings with the university.

The board of governors was a highly homogenous body. Almost all the governors were jurists, and many were alumni of the university. They were mature in years (with an average age of over fifty) and it was common for governors to remain in office for over ten years. Over half were of noble lineage. Some three-quarters of governors held political office. Despite all these factors, and this august body's indisputable authority, its influence declined. At the end of the nineteenth century, faculties – or more specifically, professors – acquired a dominant say in appointments. Furthermore, the university underwent rapid growth in this period. Given that the board of governors convened less than once a month and had to make do with only one permanent secretary, it was bound to fall short of what was required.

The main problem was that the governors were essentially outsiders. In 1922, Huizinga likened the university to a large and complex company that had no board of directors but only a supervisory board – one that moreover lacked the proper expertise. 'A mediating muffler' was his unflattering term for the board of governors. Huizinga favoured American-style efficiency, and

▲ *Interior of the senate chamber, c. 1920*

he suggested making the board of governors into an internal university body, headed by a salaried president with a large office, who would be the university's leading figure. He was eventually to have his way, but not until many years later.

The process of accelerated change after 1960 did away with the old division of tasks (*duplex ordo*) between board of governors and senate, in which the latter was responsible for the courses and the students, teaching and research. As the university expanded, the senate became too slow and the tasks too complex. The inter-university consultative Academic Council proposed replacing the old structure with two new bodies: a management top with ultimate responsibility for policy and a general consultative board including professional faculty deans. Another element of its proposal was a new university council, composed of representatives of the academic staff, students and alumni.

In the ensuing debate, senate and students clashed head-on. While the senate had no objection to better administration and greater efficiency, it insisted on faculties retaining the power to pursue their own policy in colle-

▲ *Interior of the university library, c. 1900*

giate administrative structures. The students, radicalised in the wake of international trends, demanded a far greater say in decision-making and sought the politicisation of the university. Two diametrically opposed views were at stake: the university as a goal-oriented institution for education and research, hierarchical in structure and based on expertise, versus the university as a community within which all who lived and worked were entitled to participate in the decision-making processes. Efficiency or democracy – that was the bottom line. Passionate debate on these issues would rage throughout the 1960s, with students staging numerous actions to press home their demands.

By the time the dust had settled, the higher education landscape had acquired a new piece of legislation, the University Administration (Reform) Act (WUB), which was adopted by parliament in September 1970. The most radical element of the WUB was the abolition of the senate and the introduction of a system of democratically elected councils, headed by a university council with the power to draw up a plan for the development of the university and to adopt the budget. The old boards of governors too were abolished and replaced by an executive board. While the passage of the WUB brought a turbulent period of student activism to an end, it introduced a more extreme measure of self-government than many of those involved had envisaged or desired. Furthermore, much of the efficiency gained through the introduction of an executive board was cancelled out by the political divisions that crippled the university council.

Infrastructure: The Old Institutions

It is in the university's infrastructure that the theme of freedom and restraint stands out most plainly. Helped by the economic prosperity of the latter half of the nineteenth century and constrained by the growing emphasis on specialisation and research, the university burgeoned from a single large building and a few obscure little lecture rooms into a complex of collections and institutes, libraries and laboratories. This expanding universe was rapidly becoming harder to oversee, and sustaining it meant sending constant begging letters to the central government.

An interesting tale of university architecture emerges from the plans that fell through. The main university building, for instance, attracted one visionary project after another, but in the end nothing was to supersede the intimate little church on Rapenburg canal. Yet these plans did reflect a certain idealised concept of a university. When the architects Van der Hart, Thibault and Van Westenhout were commissioned in 1809 to design a building to fill the hole that the calamitous explosion of a gunpowder ship had blown in the heart of the city two years earlier, Huizinga envisaged 'a piece of Napoleonic Paris ... flawless, self-contained and well-planned.'

> The main university building should contain everything that an
> institution of higher education might be thought ever to need:
> lecture-rooms, including an imposing, large auditorium with splendid
> royal boxes for the king and his retinue, meeting rooms, library,
> reading rooms, an anatomy theatre, an instrument room for physics,
> galleries surrounding the quadrangle, while art dealers and book-
> sellers would be expected to set up their stalls beneath the colonnades.

This project foundered for lack of funds. More importantly, perhaps, the university itself now had other aspirations. Rather than erecting an 'ostentatious building to adorn the city and the university', the board of governors preferred to spend the available money on the 'utterly indispensable expansion of scientific collections without which the university would be unable to hold its own among the learned communities of Europe.' The building debate flared up again in 1875, as the university celebrated its three-hundredth anniversary. Many new plans cast in historical style ensued. Once again, the aim was to build a symbolic edifice as well as an administrative centre. By then, however, the university saw itself rather as a collection of more or less independent institutes and laboratories.

At the end of the eighteenth century, the university's most important institutes were its collections of scientific instruments, which were expanded

in the course of the nineteenth century into impressive museums. 'Big science' started out in Leiden as a museum discipline. Between 1818 and 1825, the building known as 'Hof van Zessen' on Rapenburg canal was purchased along with the surrounding land and converted into a museum. Initially, these premises were earmarked for natural history and antiquities as well as the university's collections of art objects and scientific instruments, but eventually the director of the Natural History Museum, C.J. Temminck, managed to secure virtually the entire building for his own field. Between 1900 and 1911, the museum even acquired a new building on the site of the gunpowder disaster (known locally as 'the Ruin'), designed by Jacobus van Lokhorst. The Mu-

▲ *Laboratory for physics, chemistry, anatomy and physiology, c. 1865*

seum of Antiquities, which had moved to Breestraat in 1837, was given the building that thus became available on Rapenburg canal. In 1937, the National Museum of Ethnography, since renamed National Museum of Ethnology, acquired premises of its own, the former Academic Hospital on Steenstraat.

All the older institutions, such as the botanical gardens, library, observatory and physics instrument-collection-cum-laboratory underwent a similar increase in scale. Between 1816 and 1819 the botanical gardens were expanded, under the inspiring directorship of Sebald Justinus Brugmans, by a substantial 8,500 square metres. As a result of the Belgian uprising and its secession from the Netherlands in 1830, the gardens gained the state herbarium from Brussels, director and all (C.L. Blume). The library too expanded in successive waves of renovation throughout the nineteenth century, with a new lobby designed by J.W. Schaap being added in 1866. Ten years earlier, in 1858, the architect Henri Camp had built the university's first real laboratory, to be used for physics, chemistry, anatomy and physiology. And in 1868 Friedrich Kaiser acquired his own observatory, also built by Camp, for which the botanical gardens had to give back some of their extra space.

These buildings designed by Camp ushered in a new phase of university architecture. From then on, local architects or contractors were no longer brought in to convert existing buildings to serve a different purpose; instead, new premises were designed to fulfil specific academic or research needs. Henri Camp, since 1849 the 'King's Architect', favoured an eclectic, neo-classical style. With their tranquil, harmonious façades, his buildings exuded an ambience that accorded perfectly with the late eighteenth-century, classical concept of science and with a university that sought to produce well-rounded citizens with a broad general education.

Curiously, some of those directly responsible were disinclined to use these institutes for education. The major state museums were mainly interested in accumulating objects of scientific and scholarly interest. Furthermore, as time went on they tended to see themselves more as national institutions rather than as parts of the university. The university library too was only open for a few hours a week, and the observatory and the large laboratory focused far more heavily on research than on teaching. What is more, the

▲ *Observatory, 1861*
▼ *Observatory, 1861*
▶ *Interior of the Observatory, 1861*

premises once occupied by the Walloon Orphanage (Walenweeshuis) on Oude Vest, which had been given to the university in 1818 to use as an academic hospital, was unsuitable for teaching purposes. It was not until 1873 that the university acquired a new hospital, also built by Camp; this building was better suited for teaching, but could not be used as a real hospital. All this meant that with a few exceptions, there was no proper link between the research and teaching responsibilities of the diverse institutes.

Infrastructure: Teaching and Research

Despite this lack of structural ties, the desire to attune teaching and research to each other grew stronger as time went on. The physicians who graduated from university in the 1860s felt the absence of a good teaching hospital, with large numbers of patients and well-equipped laboratories, far more keenly than the previous generation. By then, the university as a purely educational institution was an idea to which most professors no longer subscribed. With the passage of the 1876 Higher Education Act, not just the field of education but the entire gamut of university institutes underwent substantial expansion.

The Zootomic Laboratory, built on the site of the gunpowder explosion, was an institute that had opened in 1874, before this new legislation entered into effect. This building, designed by Johan Frederik Metzelaar, still had certain features reminiscent of the older laboratories, but also included elements of the Old Dutch style that was starting to dominate architecture. In 1876 a new building for biology, located in the drive leading to the observatory, was ready for use. And the following year the then Chief Government Architect, K. de Boer, built a four-storey structure adjoining the library, on the north side of the Faliebegijn Church. In 1885 a book repository was added at right-angles to it, leading to Rapenburg canal. All these buildings – and this was something new – took account of the needs of departmental institutes and provided facilities for seminars.

The chief government architect Van Lokhorst also adhered to the Old

Dutch style for his first Leiden laboratory, the Boerhaave laboratory for pathological anatomy near the hospital, which was also completed in 1885. In that same year, work started on the major renovation of the physics/chemistry laboratory at the 'Ruin', with two new wings to accommodate the new low temperature and cryogenic laboratory needed by Heike Kamerlingh Onnes. Physiology (presided over by Willem Einthoven) acquired a laboratory in the same complex, on Zonneveldstraat.

Of greater architectural interest was the complex of three laboratories for chemistry and pharmaceutics, also designed by Van Lokhorst, just outside the old city moat on the estate of Vreewijk, which arose between 1898 and 1901. In 1899 the main university building acquired a new wing containing lecture-halls on Nonnensteeg, to which Van Lokhorst appended a new botanical laboratory in 1908. All these structures were designed in neo-Gothic style, which provided far more scope for a rational, applications-based design than the austere classicism of the past, besides which it echoed the corporate ideas of the age, which – with William Morris in their vanguard – were highly influential among the Protestant community. The renewed interest in mediaeval ideas, combined with an emphasis on the university's roots in the Middle Ages and the cohesiveness of scholarship, not just internally but also with the surrounding society, made neo-Gothicism more than just an architectural style: it encompassed an idealised vision of a university.

To a large extent these institutes were equipped for research purposes, thus reflecting the new theory of knowledge that had taken root over the previous few years. But they were also intended to be used for education, or rather for the combination of research and education that had likewise won widespread acceptance. The bold ambitions this implied first became visible in Leiden in the building of its *cité médicale* in what had become known as the Boerhaave quarter.

This site lay on the other side of the railway tracks, which for the university meant a crucial move beyond its traditional district. It also meant an experiment with the 'pavilion system', a kind of architecture used mainly in Germany. The hospital was divided into ten separate buildings: I. Administration and nursing; II. Machinery, kitchen and laundry; III. Surgery; IV. Obstetrics

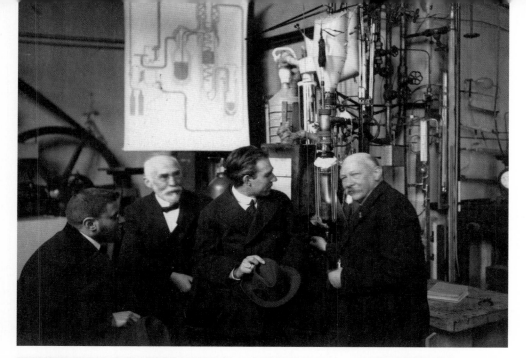

◄   *Einstein, Ehrenfest, De Sitter, Eddington and Lorentz, 1923*
▲   *Ehrenfest, Lorentz, Bohr and Kamerlingh Onnes with the second helium liquefier, 1919*
▼   *Kamerlingh Onnes and Lorentz, 1908*

and gynaecology; v. Internal medicine; vi. Infectious diseases; vii. Paediatrics; viii. Dermatology and otorhinolaryngology; ix. Ophthalmology; and x. Psychiatry. Construction work began in 1912. Such were the magnitude of this complex and the difficulty of financing it that Building x was not completed until 1955! Another lone statistic brings home the problems caused by the decentralised pavilion system: it was calculated that personnel covered a total of 327 kilometres every day just walking from one building to another.

No less radical were new proposals to address the shortage of student housing. In 1920, the 'Student village' foundation was set up, its aim being to build a 'student garden city' that would initially accommodate 128 students, based on a design by the renowned architect K.P.C. de Bazel. The project never progressed beyond the design stage, but its ambitious scale and the ideal it represented are significant in themselves. When the Student Housing Foundation was finally set up many years later, after the Second World War, it started by purchasing the large buildings Oude Vest 35 and 'Het Wallon', each of which could accommodate 50 students. The Leiden Student Housing Foundation, created in 1957, focused on creating new halls of residence: the well-known 'Sterflat' was opened in 1960, followed a little later by 'Het Hogerhuis', 'Poddekenpoel' and 'Pelikaanhof'.

Appointments and Relations

In the course of the nineteenth century, Leiden University gradually acquired a more forward-looking appointments policy. In the early nineteenth century, appointments were still the sole concern of the board of governors, and the emphasis remained on a balanced representation of the various disciplines. But around the mid-century mark, the governors gradually yielded control: the retiring professor, the faculty, and the interior minister became the key players. This meant that internal, specialist considerations moved to the fore. The appointment was still a faculty affair, but at the same time, a system of professorships started to emerge.

The most important impulse in the development of this system, of course, was the trend towards specialisation. The number of appointments per quarter-century exhibits spectacular growth: 47 between 1900 and 1924, 104 between 1925 and 1949, and 352 between 1950 and 1975. At least as striking is the average age at appointment. In the period 1875-1884 it was 26, rising subsequently to 34.9 (1895-1904), 40.4 (1925-1934) and at length 46.1 (1965-1974). As a result, the average duration of a professorship declined, in these same decades, from 45 to 28.3 years, then 25.4, and finally 11.3 years. So specialisation meant a longer wait before being appointed to a chair, but also loosened the ties between a professor and his university.

The changing composition of the team of professors is also reflected in the places where they gained their doctorates. Between 1895 and 1904, two of the professors appointed in that decade gained a doctorate abroad, while another two did so at a different Dutch university and four in Leiden. In 1925-1934 the corresponding figures were 4, 13 and 17; and in 1965-1974 they were 32, 59 and

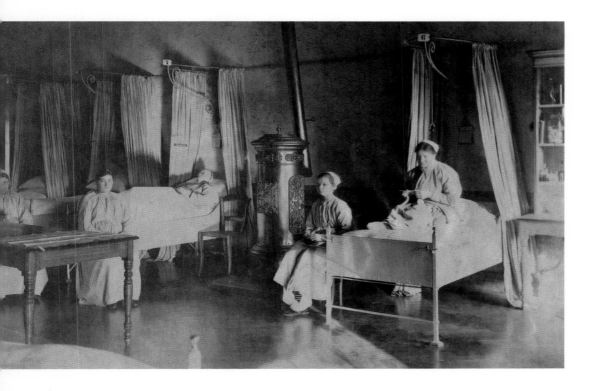

▲ *Interior of the Academic Hospital, 1889*

69. Even so, the majority of Leiden's professors were still Dutch. In the hundred years since 1875, most 'foreigners' came from the Dutch East Indies (26), followed by 16 Germans, 12 Americans, 7 Belgians. Then there were a number of Swiss (5), Frenchmen, Czechs and Italians (4 each), British, Danes, Austrians and Poles (3 each), Norwegians, South Africans and Swedes (2) and another 7 individuals from other countries.

Initially the academic staff was fairly small, comprising a select company of directors and curators, observers and assistants. A few figures may serve to illustrate the point: in 1875 Leiden's academic staff numbered 23 in total. In 1900 the institutes employed an academic staff totalling 51, besides the university's 54 professors and its 15 senior lecturers (*lectoren*) and private teachers. By 1940 the university had a total of 436 public servants, including 79 professors and 84 senior lecturers, other lecturers and professors by special appointment. Staffing necessarily kept pace with rising student numbers. In 1950 the university employed 137 teaching staff out of 771 public servants in total; the corresponding figures for 1960 were 227 and 1,751. The enormous increase in student numbers in the 1960s meant that by 1975 the university had 3,291 public servants, of whom only 1,521 were academic staff.

In the early years, these numbers played no role in the internal balance of power. Of far greater relevance to the nature and intensity of internal relations was the senate's self-image, which derived to a large extent from views concerning the purpose and function of a university. As the encyclopaedic and generalist notions of university education gradually made way for a belief in a more professional or subject-based organisation, professors became more self-assured, which altered their relations with the board of governors and the student body.

At the beginning of the nineteenth century, relations between professors and the board of governors were unequivocally bad. The aristocratic tone of *hauteur* that the board of governors adopted toward the burgher professors sowed deep resentment. 'Pedantic Guards of Zion' was how the jurist Van Assen used to describe the governors; he suspected that even the list of subjects taught was beyond their comprehension. His contempt for the governors was shared by many of his colleagues. By the end of the century, these relations were much the same, but the balance of power had swung the other way. The senate now radiated far greater self-assurance. The professors stressed the need for an organisation that was capable of responding more rapidly to trends in research and society. They wanted a greater say in the decision-making and more autonomy in relation to the ministry.

Relations between professors and students were initially formal and rather remote. The senate saw student life as a self-contained domain. Their students' internal *mores* and their conduct vis-à-vis the outside world were respected as much as possible, and where necessary, corrected with fatherly admonitions. Informal contacts did exist, though they were largely confined to a tradition whereby groups of students would descend on the professor's study for tea and biscuits, and stilted comments on the weather would be separated by long silences. In the mid-nineteenth century, the senate started intervening more actively in student life. Stiff measures were devised to encourage more studious habits, such as the *consilium abeundi*, a compelling recommendation issued to a failing student to leave the university. Ragging and initiation rituals, internal divisions between rich and poor, fraternity and non-fraternity members, were obdurate problems often discussed at senate meetings.

In lectures, too, there was a gradually change in student-teacher relations. In the first half of the nineteenth century, lectures were still conducted in Latin, even though most students had difficulty following what was said. To ease matters, the professors frequently resorted to dictation. Not until the 1860s, when faltering dictations in Latin were superseded by a freer delivery in the vernacular, did things begin to improve. Towards the end of the century, the senate sought to introduce more intensive teaching methods. The aim was to have general subjects dealt with by 'crammers' or to replace them by textbooks, conducting the true university education in small tutorial sessions or supervised sessions in the laboratory.

▲ *Orangery and hothouse in the Botanical Gardens, 1866*

▼ *Pond in the Botanical Gardens, 1866*

The Senate

Mutual relations between professors were also characterised by a certain distance throughout the nineteenth century. Differences of opinion regarding the university's aims – elitist or accessible, academic or professional – could provoke fierce exchanges at times. When we also recall the discrepancies that existed in terms of salaries, tuition fees and supplementary income, differences between liberals and conservatives, and divisions not only between members of different religious denominations but also between those who saw the Bible as the Holy Word of God and those who had tasted the forbidden fruit of biblical criticism, this distance becomes eminently understandable.

These differences were socially cushioned, it should be said, by similar middle-class lifestyles and a shared belief that academic life should possess a quality of camaraderie. In the course of the nineteenth century, there was a growing trend towards material, political and religious homogeneity. Similar neighbourhoods and homes, a liberal consensus, and religious beliefs that had converged within the limits of rationalism and agnosticism, knitted the senate together. On the other hand, the professors were now more diverse in terms of social background. Around 1800, two-thirds came from the intelligentsia; their fathers had been professors or Church ministers, teachers, physicians and so forth. This proportion fell to 57 per cent around the mid-century mark and to 52 per cent by the end of the century. In this latter period, 34 per cent of professors came from the class of middle-class property-owners, some of them even from the petty bourgeoisie, including shopkeepers, a smith, and even a street vendor. Of the 75 professors who were attached to the university in 1933, 23 came from the highest echelons of society, 36 from the middle classes, and 16 from the lower reaches of society.

At the same time, the complacency of professors spiralled to unprecedented heights. 'Today, many see a professorship as the ultimate goal', wrote the Leiden philosopher Arthur de Sopper. 'For many years now, life has been dominated by the cult of scholars.' Still, the professors were unhappy that too little heed was paid to their views. This was a frequent chorus at select gatherings, and their grievances were many. Education came first: new students had not been properly trained, many were only interested in acquiring a ticket to a profession, and a surplus of academics was looming. But the professors' discontent extended to political conditions and the culture as a whole. They fell prey to a fairly universal cultural pessimism, as expressed most famously by Huizinga in his book *In the Shadow of Tomorrow*: 'The spirit is dissipated … Like the smell of asphalt and petrol that hangs above a city, a cloud of verbosity hovers over the world.'

Against this background, during the Second World War the Leiden professors forged plans for the organisational structure and goals of the post-war university that were as detailed as they were utopian. They wanted greater independence and better administration, which they hoped to achieve by abolishing the board of governors, and introducing a university executive elected from the senate, presided over by a *rector magnificus* to hold office for five years. A supervisory board would take over the monitoring role presently fulfilled by the ministry, while a university council would retain the active participation of alumni. They also proposed practical measures to increase internal unity, such as the founding of a *Civitas* house – a building designated as a meeting-place for the entire academic community – to promote informal contact between staff and students, and a permanent general studies course, dealing with 'life issues' and a wide range of general topics. Detailed plans for sports and housing, recreation and health care were also discussed.

But the plans devised by the remaining academic staff, who met in small groups, were the most radical. While their existence had only been acknowledged in the professors' proposals in a few mildly feudal references, the lecturers themselves demanded to be heard; they submitted three reports, in which the term 'academic staff' was used for the first time. Still more radical was the *place* in which they wished to be heard: in a university council, which, unlike that proposed by the professors, would be 'a representative body for the entire academic community' and as such, the true centre of the university's power. All of these proposals contained ample material for many years of debate after the war.

▶   *Grave relief from Smyrna, 2nd century* BC

▲   *Birds in a drawer*

Science

Scientific method was born in the nineteenth century. From the classical model of knowledge that took shape in the eighteenth century, through the important intermediate stage of museological science, there was a gradual development towards science as it is understood today, defined by the crucial link between theory and experiment. Classical science revolved around collections and classification, and relied to a large extent on lay patronage. Around 1800, it was superseded by a larger-scale, more professional model of science employing analytical and comparative methods and practised in leading museums and hospitals. Around 1860, this in turn made way for a kind of activity that was based in laboratories, mainly university laboratories, oriented materially towards manipulation and control and methodologically towards quantification and precision.

In practice, hybrid forms predominated. Classical concepts of cohesiveness and harmony, order and measure, reigned supreme in Leiden well into the nineteenth century. Many continued to see science as an erudite pastime, an encyclopaedic form of fun. Every subject studied by science exhibited a self-evident unity, just as all sciences together constituted a harmonious whole. The cohesiveness that characterised this whole was God-given. It made of reality a rational amalgam, a total entity fashioned for the benefit of humankind. This implied the existence of a relationship between description and prescription, between appearance and essence. It meant that every man of science was also a philosopher, someone who used his science to demonstrate the purposefulness of God's creation, the usefulness of its creatures, and the progress made by his most important creation, Man.

Against this background, every science had its own object and objective. Natural history, as practised by internationally esteemed scholars such as Brugmans, Reinwardt and Jan van der Hoeven, was held in the highest regard in the faculty of mathematics and natural sciences. In natural history, the efficiency of God's creation, its order and its hierarchy, were perfectly plain to see. This was the subject that described the Creator's omnipotence and the central position in it of human beings. Physicians were essentially scientists who studied human beings. Medical scholars such as Macquelin and Pruys van der Hoeven (Jan's brother), while not as famous as their fellows in natural history, held the same convictions. They did not confine themselves to studying a disease, nor even to the diseased patient, but widened their scope to human beings in general. The dominant theological line, as represented by Van Voorst and Clarisse, embraced 'supranaturalism', a form of religious common sense, the belief that while the affairs of God might well transcend reason, they could never be at odds with it.

The humanities faculty was mainly concerned with moulding harmonious personalities, and taught students how to arrange – and above all how to formulate – their ideas. Big names such as Wyttenbach, Bake and Cobet upheld Leiden's reputation in philology. They sought to cultivate good taste and a sense of decorum, in which aim they were supported by their colleagues Van der Palm and Van de Wijnpersse of oriental literature and philosophy. Finally, the law faculty – which had fewer great scholars, with the possible exception of Kemper – continued in the tradition of 'elegant jurisprudence', a form of scholarship that relied on philology, the erudite intermediary between forms of life and legal system. Here, Roman law was the connecting link between jurisprudence and ancient texts.

But cracks were appearing in this harmonious edifice. Theologians were starting to question supranaturalism, although they did so behind closed doors. Elsewhere, the wind of change was blowing far more visibly: among literary scholars, men such as the archaeologist Reuvens and the orientalist Hamaker, and most notably in the writings of the jurist Johan Thorbecke. These scholars emphasised historical growth and change. To them, the status quo was not an ideal but the fossilised form of an old reality.

Around the mid-nineteenth century, scholarship as pursued by Leiden's professors was entirely dominated by the 'philosophy of experience'. Even outside the faculty of mathematics and physics, academics vied with each other in their eulogies of scientific method as the only viable method of research. Scientific activity was now ruled by the idea of development and not analogy, by progress and not the status quo.

For jurists such as Vissering, Goudsmit and Buys, this shifted the accent

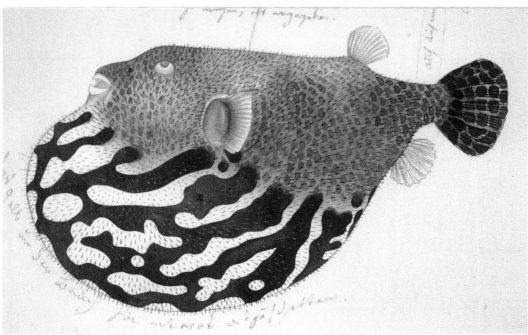

▲ *Tortoise, Von Siebold Collection*
▼ *Trunkfish, Von Siebold Collection*

▲ *Japanese crested ibis from Philip Franz von Siebold's* Fauna Japonica

squarely to the development of the constitutional state. For theologians – including such giants as Jan Hendrik Scholten and Abraham Kuenen – the historical study of the Bible moved to centre stage. In the work of men of literature such as Dozij, Juynboll and Kern (Oriental literature), Jonckbloet (Dutch), Cobet (Greek) and Fruin (history), the accent shifted from philology to history, from descriptive linguistics to dictionaries. And physicians such as Halbertsma and Schrant, Evers and Heynsius focused on physiology, on the necessity of 'force and matter'.

In the 1870s, however, other voices were raised, expressing dissatisfaction with what they saw as an unduly simplified concept of knowledge and compulsive positivism. And by the end of the nineteenth century, little remained of that watertight ideal of knowledge. Jurists (Oppenheim and Drucker, Van der Vlugt and Asser) gravitated toward concepts such as law and justice, while men of literature (De Goeje and De Groot, Ten Brink and Kalff, Muller and Blok) emphasised subjects with a prescriptive element, such as aesthetics and patriotism.

Theologians too (Tiele and Acqoy, Rauwenhoff and Gunning) were now more concerned with ethics, while physicians (Rosenstein and Van Itterson, Treub and Korteweg) concentrated on the treatment of diseased patients. Mathematicians and physicists, (Lorentz and Kamerlingh Onnes, Franchimont and Schreinemakers) primarily studied the distinction between empiricism and theory. For scholars of all disciplines, the new intellectual climate meant modifying their concept of knowledge in some way: to some it became less remote, to others more relativistic or more abstract.

Scientific Institutionalisation

With the twentieth century came a growing realisation that two dividing-lines traversed the field of academic endeavour. On the one hand, the humanities started to be viewed as distinct from the natural sciences (C.P. Snow's famous 'two cultures'), and on the other hand, a more scientistic, positivist inspiration in all academic fields was contrasted with a more empathic and more normative approach. A linguist might base his work on the strictly posi-tivist principles of the German *Junggrammatiker*, but alternatively he might adopt a far more literary or historical methodology. The influential historian P.J. Blok was greatly influenced by economic history, but the approach of his colleague Johan Huizinga was light-years away from this.

A similar tension existed in jurisprudence. In private law as well as consti-tutional and criminal law, there was all the difference in the world between theory and ideas based on positive law, between predetermined patterns and free will. While the sociologist Steinmetz in Leiden was busy explaining that every aspect of life in society was predetermined, at the other end of the spec-trum, the archaeologist A.E.J. Holwerda poked fun at all 'socio-sciences'. Lei-den economists such as Greven and Van Blom adhered unswervingly to the 'old economics' – that is, the laissez-faire school of freedom and abstract rea-soning, while all around them the new economics of social ideas and empiri-cal methods was gaining ground. In psychology, Jelgersma's complete trans-formation from a physiological psychologist into a psychoanalyst was a sign of the times.

Similar tensions existed within the exact sciences. In medicine, friction arose between practical training and courses on scientific fundamentals, with some complaining that the university was turning out physicians but not medical practitioners. Here and elsewhere, the very issue of specialisation was a separate problem. Even so, 'Boerhaave's progeny' nonetheless included important scholars such as the ophthalmologist Van der Hoeve and the psy-chiatrist Carp. In physics and chemistry, a gap opened up between the old (Newtonian) and new (Einsteinian) world view, between small-scale re-search and 'big science'. It was the age of the genius Lorentz – who arrived at university at age 16 and gained his doctorate at 21, being appointed to his first professorship three years later – who, in an exemplary working relationship with his colleague, the arch-experimentalist Kamerlingh Onnes, propelled Leiden's physics to international glory. Their achievements brought them both Nobel prizes, in 1902 and 1913, respectively. In 1924, Einthoven was simi-larly honoured for his physiology research.

The law faculty, too, went from strength to strength. In the last quarter of

▶ *Sumatra and Borneo department of the National Museum of Ethnography, c. 1900*

▲   *Pathological anatomy laboratory with statue of Boerhaave, c. 1900*

the nineteenth century, it had taken pride in great names like Buys, Goudsmit, Modderman, Van der Hoeven and Oppenheim; after the First World War, it sustained its reputation with internationally esteemed scholars such as Van Vollenhoven, Krabbe, Meijers and Van Eysinga. The traditional range of oriental studies, nourished by the collections of the university library and the Royal Institute of Linguistics and Ethnography (KITLV), gradually split along the great anthropological research lines of the *adat* specialist Van Vollenhoven, the Arabist Snouck Hurgronje, and the anthropologist De Josselin de Jong.

After the Second World War, the humanities faculty was gradually divided into Western and non-Western departments, and into 'major' and 'minor' literatures, both of which distinctions were rather unmanageable bureaucratic compartmentalisations of old linguistic or philological disciplines and 'area studies'. The law faculty retained its focus on civic responsibility, in consequence of which it offered a wide range of subdisciplines. It included a strong international section, for instance, including professorships for specialists in foreign legal systems. It also highlighted historical studies and social sciences. Thus, although the university did not have an economics faculty, it did employ several renowned economists in its law faculty. It was here, too, that Leiden's political science faculty was born.

Notwithstanding the lack of sociology, the university taught a wide range of social sciences, from cultural anthropology to psychology and educational science. Influences from both the humanities and the exact sciences, as well as questions of theory and application, continued to endow the faculty with a certain ambivalence. This was initially also true of the medical faculty, with its distinction between pre-clinical and clinical subjects. After the war, however, clinical subjects too focused more heavily on research, in surgery as well as internal medicine.

Old-fashioned though the Hugo de Groot laboratory may have been, it was soon able to accommodate the new developments in organic and physical chemistry as well as biochemistry. The physicists drew new inspiration from research into superfluidity, while the astronomers, under the brilliant leadership of Oort, mapped out the structure of our own Milky Way using spectral lines. Research in information science focused on subjects such as communicating processes, programming languages based on logic, and grammatical methods for the recognition of patterns. The biologists focused primarily on molecular botany and cell biology.

What is most striking about all these research lines is the large scale on which they were set up, something that entails an irrevocable gap in historiography. Leiden certainly had no lack of big names in this postwar period. P.A.H. de Boer and Bakhuizen van de Brink, Miskotte and Berkhof lent an unmistakeable air of distinction to the theology faculty, and Van Peursen and Nuchelmans did much the same for philosophy. Jurists such as Meijers and Van Oven, Cleveringa and Van Asbeck, Fischer and Rypperda Wierdsma, Drion and Feenstra all had formidable reputations in their respective fields. The same applied to physicians like Gorter (Evert), Rademaker, Duyff, Mulder, Querido, Van Rood, Cohen, Sobels, among others. Physicists like Kramers, C.J. Gorter, De Groot, Mazur, Kistemaker and Beenakker, and chemists like Van Arkel, Havinga, Oosterhoff, Mandel, Staverman and Ponec upheld Leiden's fame in the exact sciences, together with astronomers such as Oort and Van de Hulst, mathematicians like Kloosterman and Zoutendijk, and biologists like Lam, Kuenen, Steenis and Quispel. In the humanities, famous scholars included Duyvendak, Byvanck, De Josselin de Jong, Van Groningen, Van de Waal, Waszink, Den Boer, Milo, Dresden, Lunsingh Scheurleer, Uhlenbeck, Bachrach, Locher, Stutterheim, Van het Reve, Zürcher, Schulte Northolt, Bastet, Heesterman and De Rijk. The social sciences boasted Van Heek, Dankmeijer, Daalder and Lijphart.

Degree Courses: Structure and Aims

Under the terms of the 1815 Education Act, all new students had to complete a general foundation course: in the humanities for those seeking to study theology or law, and in mathematics and physics for aspiring medical students. Although the legislation prescribed certain subjects, it did not give details or clear definitions. There were five faculties. Following the example of France,

the philosophy faculty was split into speculative philosophy and humanities on the one hand, and mathematics and natural sciences, on the other. Subjects did not have to be taken in any set order, but a minimum period (generally three years for main subjects) was set for university attendance as a whole. The 1815 Act introduced two degrees, adding a bachelor's degree to the existing doctorate. The latter authorised the person concerned to hold certain positions in society, as described in the doctoral diploma.

In 1876, the compulsory foundation course was abolished, although medical students were still required to take a preparatory course in the natural sciences. The new Act provided for 17 specific doctorates and defined 61 subjects, the teaching of which was mandatory, as well as another 16 subjects (most of them subdisciplines of law or literature) that must be offered by at least one Dutch university. The requirements for the different doctorates were very different. The most striking discrepancy was that between the two largest branches, law and medicine. An aspiring physician seeking admission to the bachelor's examination first had to take a wide-ranging examination in the faculty of mathematics and physics. He would then prepare for the bachelor's examination in anatomy, physiology and histology, general pathology

▲ *Repository of the university library (former Faliede Bagijnkerk) in 1862*

and pharmacology. The doctoral examination included pathological anatomy, pharmaceutics, special pathology and treatment, hygienics, clinical medical practice, theoretical surgical science and theoretical obstetrics. There were additional doctoral examinations in surgery and obstetrics, and a dissertation was a compulsory part of the doctorate.

Law students, on the other hand, did not have to follow any foundation or preparatory course at all. The subjects required for their bachelor's degree were a wide-ranging course on jurisprudence, the history and fundamental principles of Roman law, and the fundamental principles of political economy. Doctoral students were examined in Dutch civil law and the fundamental principles of Dutch civil procedure, commercial law, criminal law, and the fundamental principles of Dutch criminal procedure and Dutch constitutional law. A separate doctorate in political science existed, with its own doctoral programme. And until 1921, it remained possible to obtain a doctorate in law without writing a dissertation; a list of propositions would suffice.

This difference in curricula reflected a striking discrepancy in social strategy in the country's two main professions. While the legal profession, in its efforts to influence the market, concentrated on tradition, prestige and practical training, the medical profession sought to project an image that was associated with modernity, and with the university and science in general. The main differences were in the area of doctorates. In the period 1815-1845, only 7% of Leiden's law students were awarded doctorates, but in the period 1876-1905 this proportion had soared to some 75%. In the medical faculty, we find almost the opposite trend. In the early period, 62% obtained doctorates, while in the latter period only 25% did so. By this time, dissertations in medicine had developed into fully-fledged monographs representing years of research, an initiation into a scientific élite. Law students generally produced a few pages of propositions or at most a competent compilation, 'a wordy sort of visiting-card', as one commentator puts it.

So while the law faculty was eventually awarding doctorates to three-quarters of its students, the medical faculty admitted only about one-third of its students to the 'finals' and awarded doctorates to only a quarter. The practical elements that were heavily emphasised in the medical curriculum took their toll in the examinations. Law's emphasis on theory made the academic demands relatively light. Ironically, all those doctors of law were popularly derided as donkeys, while the physicians who were so heavily drilled in practical skills, only a quarter of whom acquired doctorates, acquired an aura of scientific learning.

These differences, and the images that went with them, were not abolished until the Act of 1960, which was the product of a higher education commission that had been established in 1949. The commission proposed defining nine different areas of specialisation within law: private law, constitutional law, criminal law, and international law, as well as economic law, social law, the history and philosophy of law, notarial law, and the specialist subdiscipline of fiscal law. The ultimate aim was to divide the law school into three major disciplines: Dutch law, notarial law, and constitutional law. In all three, a master's degree conferred *civiel effect*, that is, it qualified the graduate to act in a Dutch courtroom, whether as a barrister or judge.

The medical faculty too was changing significantly. Many strongly advocated a general basic medical training, with a foundation course in biology instead of in the natural sciences. A separate course for those wanting to set up in medical practice had to contain two main subjects, internal medicine and surgery, with the possible addition of a subject that studied human beings in their totality. More striking still was the fact that the 1968 academic statute no longer described the subjects to be examined, since the field was 'in a state of constant development'. Several basic subject areas were described, eight for the bachelor's and five for the master's degree. In medicine as well as law, the degree courses marched to the tune of academic progress, and in both cases, the aim was to prepare students for 'the exercise of positions in society requiring academic training'.

Students: Numbers and Background

First of all, let us review the numbers. Between 1775 and 1812, a total of 3,379 students enrolled at the university. The largest faculty was law, with 1,270

▶ *Interior of the Minerva Society, 1829-1830*

students, followed by medicine (953) and theology (692), while the humanities were by far the smallest faculty (314). Interestingly, there was only a modest increase in total student numbers (4,003) for the period 1815 to 1845, but the largest faculties were now law (1,634) and theology (1,108), followed by medicine (992), humanities (222), and mathematics and physics (47). Over the following thirty years, with 4,214 registered students, law remained the largest faculty (1,987), but medicine (853) edged ahead of theology (835). The humanities scarcely grew at all (287), but mathematics and physics underwent rapid growth (252).

These figures mainly bear witness to the political confusion of the years under French rule, but they also reflect the greater appeal that the 1815 legislation had imparted to higher education. The grants system it had introduced, and the exemption from tuition fees that applied to theology students for several decades, were initially a powerful boost to student numbers. So, in the early years, we see that the majority of students opted for either law or theology, the former being traditionally the largest faculty while the latter was subject to artificial inflation.

Another circumstance that attracted students to the university was the relatively benevolent examination system: between 60 to 70 per cent of all students completed their course. One factor that played a role here was the encyclopaedic, didactic principles underlying the teaching system, with an emphasis on attending lectures rather than on passing examinations, on moulding minds rather than training specific skills. Most university students during this period had fathers with occupations in the sphere of law or administration, and most came from the upper echelons of society. In all respects, the early nineteenth century simply prolonged the *ancien régime*.

The mid-nineteenth century brought a change in this situation. Since theologians were being enticed away to the more conservative Utrecht, and medical students were flocking to the new clinical schools, Leiden University became almost exclusively a legal faculty. It also introduced stricter examinations (even more so in medicine than in law), as a consequence of changing views regarding the aims of higher education (more geared towards practice) and about professionalism.

▶ *Self-portrait of Eduard Stollé, member of the 'Leidse Jagers', 1831*

▲ *Front façade of the Minerva Society on Rapenburg canal, c. 1840*
▼ *The Minerva Society's garden side on Rapenburg, c. 1840*

It was around this time that we see a radical change in the social composition of the student population: from the 1860s onwards, Leiden University recruited half or more of its students from the lower middle classes. 'Many retailers and shopkeepers whose businesses are flourishing consider their sons too good for such humble employment and send them to university, full of illusions of a brilliant future,' complained the Leiden mathematician Van Geer in 1887. In this period of economic growth, optimistic expectations of the future prompted small tradesmen to send at least one of their sons to university.

The social background of the students – the enormous influx of the children of secondary school teachers, shopkeepers and public servants, and growing numbers of students with fathers working in trade and industry – is another sign that universities were starting to react to economic trends in nineteenth-century society. This means that universities should not be seen in this period as bodies that strengthened the elite and widened existing social divisions, but quite the contrary, certainly in the latter half of the century, as instruments of social advancement that helped to defuse the social tension generated by economic change.

The most important changes date, of course, from the Higher Education Act of 1876. The new Act does not initially appear to have had any marked impact on actual student numbers, however. With fewer than 5,000 students in the period 1875-1905, the university as a whole appears to have stagnated, but this may be partly because the vast majority of students from Amsterdam, who had been unable to graduate from their local college, the *Atheneum Illustre*, under the old legislation, were able to do so after the college was upgraded to university status in 1876 and therefore no longer needed to transfer to Leiden. The stagnation was most apparent in the law faculty (with 1,998 students), but medicine enjoyed explosive growth (1,428), while theology declined just as sharply (409). Student numbers in the humanities (527) and mathematics and physics (428) almost doubled in this period.

Not until after 1925 did student numbers really soar. That year, the student almanac records the presence of 2,493 students (88 in theology, 882 studying law, 625 medicine, 429 mathematics and physics, 209 humanities and philosophy and 260 training to become officials in the Dutch East Indies). In 1960 the

▲ *J. Robert, beadle of Leiden Student Fraternity, 1854*
▼ *J.C. Emeis, assistant to the student society Minerva, 1854*

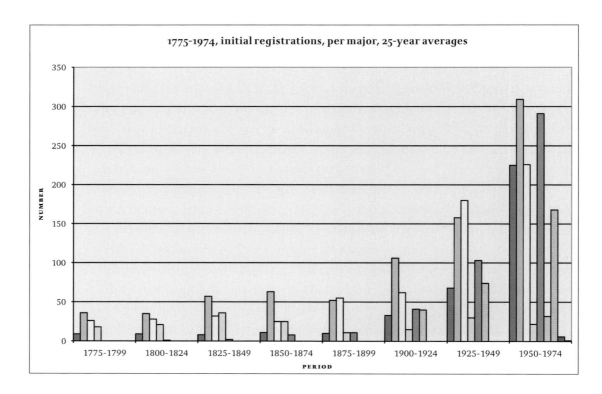

1775-1974, initial registrations, per major, 25-year averages

Legend: Humanities, Law, Medicine, Theology, Math.&Physics, Law&Hum., Social Sciences, Philosophy, Archaeology

total number of registered students was 5,027 (106 in theology, 954 in law, 1,216 in medicine, 1,238 mathematics and physics, 978 humanities and philosophy, and 535 in so-called 'joint faculties' of law, humanities and philosophy). Around the First World War, around one-eighth of the students were women, but this proportion had risen to over a quarter by the outbreak of the Second World War, an average that remained stable for many years after the war.

Student numbers gradually doubled between 1945 and 1960: from 2,824 (2,111 men and 713 women) to 5,370 (3,723 men and 1,647 women). But then they took only one decade to double again (11,858 in 1970: 8,159 men and 3,699 women) After this, the number of male students remained fairly constant (almost 9,000 in 1985), but the number of women continued to rise until it equalled the number of men, so that in the academic year 1985-86, almost 18,000 students were enrolled, the largest number ever registered at Leiden.

The choice of course displayed an equally remarkable shift. The substantial decline in law and medicine, the corresponding growth in the humanities – and the still more striking growth in the social sciences and in mathematics and physics – transformed Leiden's student population, which had traditionally been dominated by future doctors and lawyers, but which were now evenly divided among the university's five large areas of learning.

The explosive rise in student numbers, in Leiden and elsewhere, was accompanied by two noteworthy side effects, namely a decline in the proportion of graduates and a decline in the level of participation in organised student life. The growing drop-out rate, identified by the government agency Statistics Netherlands in its report for 1962, aroused considerable public concern. After five years at university, it appeared that only about half of the students had passed their bachelor's examinations and almost 40% never obtained a master's degree. Most of the blame was laid on the one-sided academic emphasis of teaching, and some observers proposed setting up university education on the principles applied in English-speaking countries, differentiating between two kinds of degree courses, a practically-oriented type, shorter than the existing master's degree courses, and a separate type of course for those wishing to pursue academic careers.

The following year, the minister submitted a proposal, having first consulted the Academic Council, to shorten degree courses by altering the course structure and reducing the quantity of material covered. The proposal envisaged courses lasting five years in total, composed of a baccalaureate for all incoming students and an advanced programme for aspiring academics. The proposal met with protests from the entire academic community, but it was most notably, perhaps, the starting signal for the launch of the student union, which was greatly boosted by the first rise in tuition fees in 1964. A clash between different interest groups went hand in hand with a process of consciousness-raising, resulting in the loss of traditional fraternity activities.

The fall in fraternity membership had already attracted attention before that. The increase in the number of students from the working classes (18% in 1974, while almost 50% came from the lower middle classes), the relatively greater increase in faculties with little interest in traditional forms of frater-

nity fun (mathematics and physics, sociology); all such factors increased the number of students who declined to join student fraternities, a phenomenon so dreaded that it was known in Leiden jargon as 'nihilism'. The ageing of the student population, the increase in numbers of married students, and growing numbers of students who commuted from another town or combined their studies with paid employment, were other contributory factors. The fragmentation of the student population, with the loss of what had once been a closely-knit *civitas*, was now a fact of life.

Student Life

At the end of the eighteenth century, deep divisions among Leiden's student population sparked a process of regrouping and reorganisation. These divisions were primarily social, and their most visible expression was in the ragging that accompanied initiation, rituals devised to introduce newcomers to the student community. Initiation would be the primary catalyst among students throughout the nineteenth century. Initially the custom was mainly a source of discord, but it was a scandal involving ragging, in 1839, that led to the official founding of the student fraternity, an autonomous organisation that was eventually sanctioned by the university senate and whose membership included virtually all students.

The fraternity's launch certainly did not end the excesses of ragging; on the contrary, fresh scandals erupted virtually every year. Most complaints revolved around violent treatment and the forced consumption of large quantities of alcohol, besides which the hapless newcomers were required to undergo sexual 'rites of passage' in which they were confronted with new items of vocabulary and taught certain practical skills in the shortest possible time. The test that concluded this period of torment took the form of an 'initiation play' in which obscenity loomed large. In 1911, when the Leiden Chinese scholar De Groot published the script of one of these plays, the ensuing scandal prompted days of debate in Parliament and heated arguments in the university senate, culminating in De Groot's departure to Berlin.

▲ *Leiden student in the 1840s*

The fraternity's main organisational feature, besides the fact that it ran its own clubhouse, complete with bar, dining room tables and a library, was the plethora of auxiliary societies it spawned. These ranged from sports clubs to regional associations (for students of the same geographical origin), but the most important were the clubs formed within each new cohort of students and the debating societies. The former, set up by the newcomers themselves, tended to divide along lines of social background, with each new student being assigned a mentor, someone from a higher year who helped introduce him to student life.

The debating societies were more distinctive still and actually predated the fraternity, the first ones having been founded in the early nineteenth century. Just as the fraternity's organisational structure mimicked that of the

▲ *Franz Liszt being welcomed to Leiden, 1843*

professorial senate, some of its activities mimicked lectures. The earliest debating societies were literary groups, but these were soon joined by others that were subject-based. Most debating societies were relatively small, with about ten members, and met every two weeks, at around 6 p.m. Each had its own baize-upholstered lectern (spattered with ink, wine and candle-wax) and a document-chest with its internal code of conduct and the minutes of its meetings. The evening would generally be divided into two parts, an oration with an appraisal and the defence of a number of propositions, followed by drinks galore and late-night snacks. Throughout the debating session, copious fines would be dished out for violations of the code of conduct – for speaking too long or not long enough, for interrupting, and so on. The fines went into a fund to pay for the society's annual outing. Members would also meet for purely social occasions, on Sunday afternoons or weekdays at 6 p.m. for instance, to enjoy hot chocolate and rusks, gin and bitters and glasses of Madeira.

Besides all this, the students were also an active force in society at large. Most notably perhaps, this social involvement ran to a willingness to take up arms in times of political unrest. In 1784, the students formed a militia, Pro Pallade et Libertate, to protect fraternity members from the Orangist rabble. A group formed in 1815, the Flankeurs, made a last-ditch attempt to repel Napoleon's forces at Waterloo. While these represented small pockets of enthusiasm, when the king called upon his people to take up arms against the Belgians in 1830, one-third of the entire student fraternity enlisted, partly from nationalist motives and partly enticed by what the student poet (and corporal) Gerrit van de Linde would call the 'virgin-seducing green and yellow military uniforms'. In 1848, the students established a corps of Preservers of the Peace, and in 1866 the Prussian threat prompted the founding of Pro Patria, a student militia that enjoyed widespread support among the professors. In 1914, the Leiden Student Volunteer Corps was formed.

One of the most fascinating events in student life was undoubtedly the masquerade, a costumed procession held every five years, starting in the nineteenth century, as part of the university's anniversary celebrations. Four key strands can be distinguished in the masquerade's developmental history.

◄ *Moeke Nieuwenhuis, the 'coffee lady', c. 1900*

In the first place, there was a growing emphasis on historical accuracy, which meant that more and more documentary sources and experts were consulted with the passage of time. Secondly, the costumes became ever more magnificent and elaborate. This trend was fostered by a change in planning from 1850 onwards; instead of being held on an evening in February, the procession was moved to an afternoon in June. Then there was the factor of national sentiment. There was a growing insistence on placing national identity at the heart of the masquerade, and more specifically on choosing a member of the House of Orange as the main character. Finally, there was the question of morality, of the examples set by the figures.

At the end of the nineteenth century, historical inspiration faded into the background, to be replaced by stylised ostentation. The masquerade became a *Gesammtkunstwerk*, with dramatic performances and magnificent structures. As time went on, the masquerade was organised more and more by specialist theatre experts, with numerous supporting roles being played by hired extras. At the beginning of the twentieth century, it developed into a grand spectacle that lasted a week and attracted visitors from far and wide, but at the same time, it dug its own financial grave, and could not be sustained during the Great Depression of the 1930s.

Fraternity-based events, even those organised on as large a scale as the masquerade, could not conceal the fact that the student fraternity was disintegrating by the late nineteenth century. This was partly because of growing numbers of 'nihilists', students who did not join the fraternity. Even the senate considered this to be a worrying trend, since the professors also saw that much of the students' socialisation and education took place in fraternity life. Another trend was one of separation along religious and other lines. In 1893, the Catholic student fraternity Sanctus Augustinus was founded, followed in 1901 by a Protestant equivalent, Societas Studiosorum Reformatorum (SSR). Meanwhile, in 1900, Leiden had also acquired its own society for women students (the VVSL). In 1911, the Federation of Leiden Students was formed; in 1930 it merged with Unitas Studiosorum Lugduno-Batava, a mixed society that did not have initiation rituals. Socialising 'among your own kind' became the watchword. Social clubs of this kind tended to take little interest in poli-

▲ *Senior student on the lookout for new 'green' undergraduates, c. 1920*
▼ *Student with* paranimfen *[those who accompany and support a PhD student on the day of the award ceremony] on their way to the PhD award ceremony, c. 1920*

▲ *The premises of the student society Minerva, Breestraat, just after its completion in 1876*

tics, although there was widespread support for the 'Great Netherlands' ideal. Enthusiasm initially focused on South Africa and the Boers in Transvaal. Later on, the students' hearts warmed up to the Flemish movement. Many were also eager to play a part in the international peace movement.

Party politics, in the sense of a commitment to socialist or liberal ideas, was avoided as much as possible. For a short time, the widening gap between rich and poor polarised opinions, and some took to tearing up socialist periodicals to which the student club had a subscription: the prevailing mood was against politics, especially the politics of social divisions. Fraternity politics was admissible, but other subjects tended to be shunned, on the principle of 'Every man to his trade'. The behaviour of Leiden's students at the conference of the International Student Service held in Leiden in 1933 – at which the German delegation was headed by the Nazi Von Leers – was naïve, to put it mildly. When the Rector Magnificus, Johan Huizinga, refused to extend his university's hospitality to Von Leers, the students, including the fraternity representative, deplored his decision.

During the Second World War, student representatives and senate alike thought long and hard about the reorganisation of the university after the war. To restore the unity of the student community, Leiden's student fraternity sought to make people of different religious backgrounds more welcome than in the past, while Augustinus, SSR and Unitas were to be partly or completely subsumed into the LSC. The latter would become a society for the entire student community, characterised by greater religious and social openness and lower fees.

Although the plans for community-building produced some impressive results in the ten years following the war – in terms of housing and health care, wide-ranging general interest courses, canteens and sports facilities, and an academic arts centre – by the early 1950s, the idea was already losing its appeal. It was above all the scale expansion and the slow but steady changes in the composition of the student body that gradually eroded its cohesiveness and, hence, its community spirit. The change can best be described in sociological terms. Instead of the social standing that had once been associated with students, on the basis of a shared traditional, hierarchical lifestyle, what now emerged was an independent class of students with similar problems and interests, pursuing similar goals.

This independent spirit soon brought them into conflict with the senate. In principle, it was mainly a question of mentality. The senate was starting to express serious concern about what it could only see as a decline in moral standards. An old, explicitly erotic play such as Schnitzler's *Reigen*, staged by a student drama club, sowed deep divisions between students and professors. But political issues too were starting to become divisive. While a commentator in Amsterdam's student paper *Propria Cures* dubbed Leiden University the 'Borobudur of the Bourgeoisie', the Dutch government's policy in New Guinea and the development of atomic energy were generating bitter controversy. Before long, issues relating to every corner of the earth – Central America, North Africa, Southeast Asia – were providing food for indignation.

Thus, even sedate Leiden became the setting for 'happenings' such as those that had shaken up academic institutions in other parts of the country and around the world. Although the waves in Leiden were rather less turbulent than those in Nijmegen or Amsterdam, the main university building was nonetheless occupied from 8 to 20 May 1968 and used as a centre of ongoing debate and actions; even St Peter's Church found itself being requisitioned several times for these unfamiliar goings-on. The ensuing process of internal democratisation, combined with the opening-up of the old student fraternities, completely transformed student life. In 1969, the leaders of the Leiden Student Fraternity presented themselves for the first time not in morning coats, but in corduroy suits.

City, Country, and World

Town and gown, however, remained closely connected. The burgomaster was traditionally a member of the university's board of governors, many professors and students came from Leiden, and a number of the university's institutions were accessible to the general public. The museums provided edifying entertainment, the botanical gardens offered tranquillity of mind, and the observatory provided a sense of one's own insignificance and the greatness of God. Besides these relatively informal or everyday forms of interaction, there were other more institutional connections, which grew into a tightly-knit fabric linking the university to the city.

One of the first nineteenth-century institutions that operated on the interface of city and university was the technical school, founded to promote local industry. Schools of this kind had been created at the behest of King William I 'to arouse the slumbering nation and prod it into diligence.' Under the rather eccentric directorship of Professor A.H. van der Boon Mesch, students ranging from simple apprentice carpenters and smiths to practising or aspiring manufacturers and architects were initiated into the mysteries of chemistry, such as these applied to 'the arts and manufacturing'.

As the century drew on, various university institutions were embedded

▲ *Lecture given by Professor Thorbecke, who attracted large crowds, unlike many of his colleague*

V.V.S.L.

OPGERICHT

27 JANUARI

1900

more emphatically in the city's care structure. The teaching hospital, for instance, initially an obscure little ward for a few patients who were of clinical interest to students, evolved into a large, modern hospital, which admitted penniless locals as well as clinically interesting cases, on humane grounds. There were other forms of symbiosis between students and townspeople. Students participated in major local festivities, and their masquerades delighted the whole of Leiden, as well as other towns and villages for miles around. The students' literary clubs held public meetings, and Sempre Crescendo invited the local population to their musical performances. Conversely, Leiden's Charitable Society could count on the students' membership and their generosity.

Most of all, however, it was the professors who embodied, as it were, the bond between town and gown. It was they who gave a certain *cachet* to the many local literary and learned societies; their lectures served as adult education classes *avant la lettre*. In addition, every Church congregation, every school board, advisory body or charitable institution boasted several professors among its members. Every electoral college, too, contained the names of Leiden professors.

In the course of the nineteenth century, the professors' commitment to the city became far more pronounced. Published lists of local dignitaries include references to their numerous positions. There were nearly always three or more professors sitting on the city council. Not a single school or almshouse existed that did not have professors on its board. Charities set up for every conceivable purpose, from supporting fishermen's widows to building a swimming pool, from missionary societies to institutes for deaf mutes, from public health improvements to raising orphans in families, from working men's pension funds to Leiden's bread factory, were always run with the aid of university professors.

In the twentieth century, the university's sheer size made it a massive presence in the city. Not only did it become the biggest employer, but it also commissioned far more buildings than any other body. In the 1950s, plans were made to clear a large site to the west of the Academic Hospital, between Wassenaarseweg and Plesmanlaan up to Highway 44, to be occupied by a sci-

◄ *Design for the banner of the Society of Women Students at Leiden*

ence complex. At the same time, a far smaller strip was earmarked for the humanities and a new library, between Witte Singel and Rijnkade/Schiekade. The laboratories were completed in the 1960s and 1970s, and the university library opened in 1984. At the same time, old buildings were renovated and reallocated. Two were converted into legal studies centres: the Gravensteen building, which reopened in 1955, followed in 1972 by the Grotius Centre for International Legal Studies, which took possession of the former laboratories in Vreewijk.

At national level – once national unity had been established – the university acquired a special position that set it apart from other institutions. This separate status was explicitly defined in the 1815 Education Act, which noted that Leiden University, as the 'first' university in the country, should be given preferential treatment 'in grants and salaries'. The university continued to function on this basis throughout the nineteenth century and even into the early twentieth century, although the 1876 Act formally abolished its privileged position. While the sense of nationhood fostered by Leiden's professors was initially classicist, narrowly aligned with the Patriot movement, once hearts and minds had finally been won over to Romanticism, a full-blooded nationalism started throbbing through university life, transforming scholarship.

It was in the humanities, of course, that this transformation was most conspicuous. To the great linguist Matthias de Vries, language found its truest expression not in books but 'as it lives and grows in the hearts of the people, free and untrammelled, loose and lively, and yet at the same time pure and unadulterated.' The mammoth dictionary of the Dutch language that would take over a hundred years to complete, *Woordenboek der Nederlandsche Taal*, was conceived in Leiden as a 'museum of language … a treasure-house of all the riches of our mother tongue'. De Vries presided over the creation of the first chair in Dutch history, which was initially formed as a specialist offshoot of his own professorship in 1860. The underlying idea was to have a chair that would be both national and constructive, and the successive professors, Fruin and Blok, however different their approaches, patently radiated national inspiration.

Prominent themes in this nationalism were preserving national unity rather than focusing on religious differences, and highlighting culture more than politics. So Leiden's professors channelled their love of country into specific causes around 1900, such as the struggle of the Boers in South Africa and the Flemish question. Fruin's comparison of the Boers' resistance to the English with the Dutch revolt against Spain sank into the national consciousness. Virtually all of Leiden's professors belonged to the local branch of the Netherlands South Africa Association for varying periods of time. In the twentieth century, the Great Netherlands ideal would focus more on Flanders and on improving the administration of the Dutch East Indies.

Where the Dutch East Indies were concerned, the combined faculties of law and humanities passionately supported the proposed 'Ethical Policy' (which its critics derided as 'ethical blindness') that sought to modernise the colony with the aid of education and scientific advances in preparation for independence. 'The native population craves our knowledge,' said Colenbrander in 1918 in his inaugural address as professor of colonial history, 'partly, and most ardently, because it feels the need of it as a weapon to wield against the unreasonable prolongation of our domination.' Snouck Hurgronje and Van Vollenhoven, in particular, lent their resounding names to this cause, but they found themselves fighting a rearguard action against the conservative forces in Dutch society.

Such causes automatically made national inspiration international. The Netherlands' actions on the world stage had traditionally sprung from its awareness of being a small country. This small country spent much of the nineteenth century racked with doubts about its own *raison d'être*. The possibility of accepting annexation into Germany was considered in all seriousness, but the notion elicited swift rebukes, most notably from Leiden. Thorbecke, Fruin and Blok emphasised strongly that small states were centres of peace and liberty, cosmopolitan forces that must play the role of mediators in the frequently disharmonious concert of nations. While acknowledging Germany's profound influence on the Netherlands, they pointed out that the Netherlands was actually not a small but a great nation, small in surface area but great on account of its past, its colonies, and above all its achievements in scholarship.

Towards the end of the nineteenth century, the Netherlands produced several great legal minds. Besides Leiden-trained jurists such as Van Vollenhoven and Eysinga, the most noteworthy were T.M.C. Asser and J. de Louter. Their brilliant construction of international law would affirm the Netherlands' greatness (as well as its security). The same applied *a fortiori* in the natural sciences. The Nobel Prizes that descended on Dutch science like a beneficent rain, made the country, in the words of the German chemist W. Voigt, 'a great power in the realm of physics'.

It was against this background, further encouraged by the active peace movement, that a plan was forged to make The Hague the 'world capital of the intellect'. The architect De Bazel actually designed plans to realise this ambition, including a peace palace and an international academy (to be called the

▲ *University library, 1862*

Association des Académies). That Dutch academia looked kindly on this endeavour is clear from an article contributed by Lorentz in 1913 to the journal *Vrede door recht*, explaining the ways in which international research promoted peace. It was Van Vollenhoven's pamphlet *De Eendracht van het Land*, also dating from 1913, that caused the biggest stir, with its passionate insistence on the Netherlands' moral task in the world.

After the First World War, which split even the international academic community into two opposing camps, the Netherlands' Royal Academy, led by Lorentz and Van Vollenhoven, waged a fierce battle of diplomacy to reverse the expulsion of scholars from the so-called Central Powers from the recently created International Research Council. Shuttling back and forth between Berlin and Paris, they tried to arrive at a sort of 'academic Locarno'. Although this plan miscarried – after 1933, the researchers found themselves facing Nazis across the table – their efforts certainly reflect the considerable self-confidence of Dutch scientists at that time.

These efforts were inextricably linked to the autonomy of Dutch academia. In universities, even more than in political circles, admiration for Germany clashed with fears of being a satellite. 'Around 1890, Dutch academics, in every field from medicine to political science or philology, sought overwhelmingly to orient themselves in relation to Germany and the Germanic spirit,' wrote Huizinga in the 1930s. The First World War made many of Germany's erstwhile admirers in the Netherlands rethink their position. Lorentz urged the importance of small nations protecting their academic autonomy and their freedom to blossom in their own right. Once again, Van Vollenhoven was the most outspoken in his views: 'Liberating ourselves from German academia is another reflection of our quest to secure a place for ourselves in the international arena,' he wrote in 1925. Much the same applied after the Second World War, but then the quest for independence focused not on Germany but on the United States.

Even before the Second World War, major American funds such as the Carnegie Endowment and the Rockefeller Foundation tended to focus the attention of European academics – and this certainly included the Dutch – on the United States. As a Fellowship Advisor of the Rockefeller Foundation, Hu-

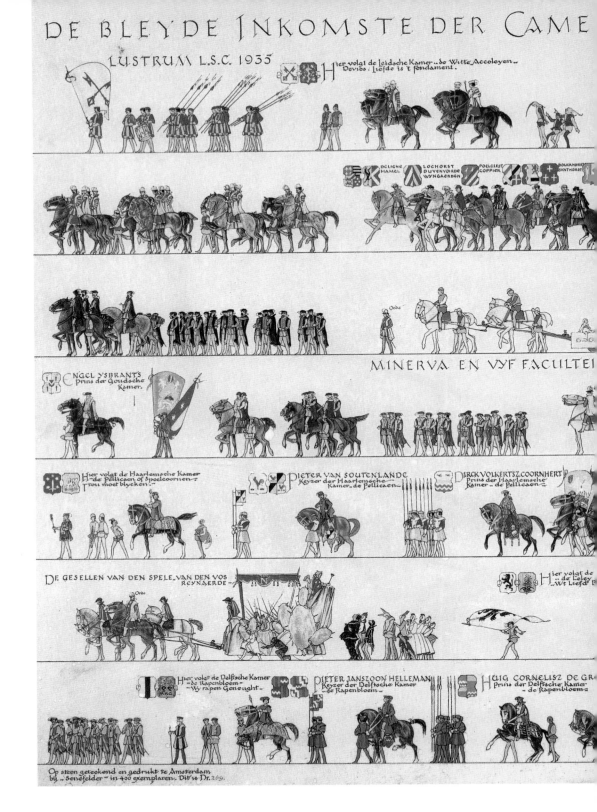

Masquerade print, 1935

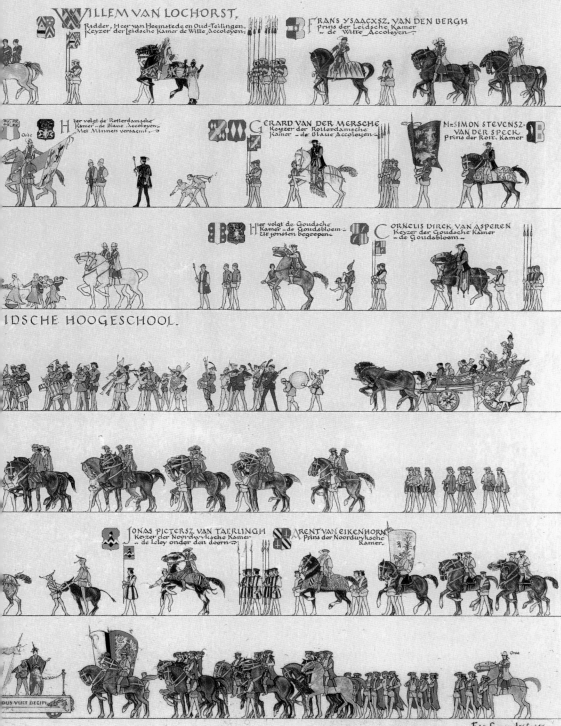

VAN RHETHORYKE BINNEN LEYDEN

WILLEM VAN LOCHORST,
Ridder, Heer van Heemstede en Oud-Teilingen,
Keyzer der Leidsche Kamer de Witte Accoleyen.

FRANS YSAACXSZ. VAN DEN BERGH
Prins der Leidsche Kamer
„de Witte Accoleyen"

Hier volgt de Rotterdamsche
Kamer „de Blaue Accoleyen"
Met Minnen versaemt.

Orde

GERARD VAN DER MERSCHE
Keyzer der Rotterdamsche
Kamer „de Blaue Accoleyen"

Mr SIMON STEVENSZ·
VAN DER SPECK
Prins der Rott. Kamer

Hier volgt de Goudsche
Kamer „de Goudsbloem"
Ut jonsten begrepen.

CORNELIS DIRCK VAN ASPEREN
Keyzer der Goudsche Kamer
„de Goudsbloem"

IDSCHE HOOGESCHOOL.

JONAS PIETERSZ VAN TAERLINGH
Keyzer der Noordwyksche Kamer
„de Leley onder den doorn"

ARENT VAN EIKENHORN
Prins der Noordwyksche
Kamer.

Orde

Frits Lensvelt fecit
1·9·3·6

izinga alerted Dutch academics to the grants being offered by the foundation, which also provided considerable financial support to Leiden's astronomy and physics departments. After the war, research was restructured, most notably with the establishment in 1950 of the Netherlands Organisation for the Advancement of Pure Research (zwo), entirely along American lines. Furthermore, the dynamics of the Fulbright Program had the effect that Dutch research became strongly oriented towards developments in the United States. The trend towards 'education for the many' and the gradual division of the research field into three major divisions – the humanities, natural sciences and social sciences – rather than the two cultures that had prevailed in the past, likewise refashioned university life, in Leiden as elsewhere, along American lines.

▲ *Detail of the masquerade, 1875*

Constraints and Liberty

Even the advent of the Kingdom and the unified national state did not immediately put paid to the university's freedom. The original draft of the 1815
education legislation retained the independent position of the board of governors, and it was only after the personal intervention of the education minister that the restrictions mentioned above concerning appointments and financial policy were introduced. The freedom of students and professors was
likewise left virtually intact. Students could study courses in any order and
take as long as they pleased to graduate. As for the professors, the Leiden legal
scholar Kemper who had drafted the new Act boasted that he had based education 'almost exclusively on the experience, preferences and opinions of
teachers themselves'.

From this it is clear that social factors greatly outweighed cognitive con-

siderations in the drafting of that legislation. 'To elevate the learned classes
once more to the position of respect they had always enjoyed in the Netherlands in the past ... that is what Kemper wanted to achieve,' wrote Huizinga.
Thus, academic freedom was part of a higher order of middle-class values.
The freedom that the university enjoyed for the next half-century was that of
the liberal (here in the sense of 'laissez-faire') 'night watchman' state. In the
words of Jan Romein: 'The only reason why the liberal state does not interfere
with the university is because it is unnecessary, and the reason why it is unnecessary is that all the professors are liberal themselves.'

This blissful state of affairs came to an end around 1900. As the government became more centralised, it concerned itself more closely with the
structure of society; in addition, that government was no longer liberal but to
a growing extent dominated by confessional forces. After his resounding victory in 1901, Abraham Kuyper, the leader of the Anti-Revolutionary Party, offered the universities greater financial autonomy along with the freedom to
introduce new professorships – some of which, of course, would have to be
based on confessional principles. But Leiden's senate declined to take the bait.
Lorentz noted at the time: 'The freedom of research and publication is much
appreciated, but the autonomy proffered along with it is not deemed indispensable. We have always rejoiced in freedom thus far without it. Who is to
say whether agreement with the proposals would not ultimately lead to a cur-
tailment of that freedom?'

It seems that academic freedom was by then defined in different terms: the
crux was no longer the autonomy of professors, but 'freedom of research and
publication'. General liberal erudition had been superseded by specialised
academic knowledge. It was the representation of that knowledge in all of its
branches and the cohesiveness of research and education that defined the
university. That was what made Kuyper's proposal so shrewd: an individual
policy on professorships was at the very heart of academic freedom. Indeed,
all universities had set up special funds of their own between 1886 and 1893,
precisely to enable them to pursue such a policy.

Huizinga saw these funds as representing 'an entirely new principle in the
administration of universities'. But the idea of American-style universities

▲ *Library lending department, 1948*

▲   *Academic Hospital, 1957*

with their own private fortunes, as cherished by Huizinga and others (such as Van Vollenhoven) would never materialise. In fact, events moved in quite the opposite direction. The 1960 Higher Education Act did invest the university with legal personality: from then on it would administer its own property, including real estate, and was permitted to amass its own capital. But the scale expansion that took place at this time removed any notion of financial independence to the realm of the imagination.

This scale expansion did lead to a redefinition of education. Research, including its integration with teaching, would henceforth be only one of its pillars. The Act also emphasised the importance of practical training and general education. And this meant that academic freedom was once more in jeopardy. By then, this freedom had been defined explicitly as freedom of research and publication. Isaiah Berlin once distinguished between two concepts of freedom: 'freedom *from* interference' and the more limited 'freedom *for* a predefined end'. This proved an apt distinction when it came to the freedom enjoyed by universities. The first kind was that referred to by Lorentz. The second kind would increasingly come to dominate the debate. It was an acrimonious debate.

SEBALD JUSTINUS BRUGMANS

ART. LIB. MAG. MED. ET PHIL. DOCT. PHIL. LOG. METAPH.
ET ASTRON. IN ACAD. FRANEQ. 1785 PROF ORD. IN ACAD.
LUGD. BAT. 1786 BOTAN. 1787 HIST. NAT. 1791 MED. 1800 CHEM
NAT. FRANEQUERAE 24 MART. 1763 OB. 22 JULII 1819.

JOHANNES RUDOLPHUS THORBECKE ZWOLLA -TRANSISALANUS

NATUS 15 JAN: Aº 1798 IN FAC: JURID: ACAD: LUGD: BAT: PROF: EXTRAORD:
Aº 1831 ORD: 1834. MINISTER REGIS FACTUS Aº 1849. OBIIT 4 JUN: Aº 1872

ABRAHAMUS KUENEN.

THEOL. ET LITT. HUM. DOCT. IN ACAD.
LUGD. BAT. THEOL. PROF. 1853–1891. NATUS HARLEMI
16 SEPT. 1828. OBIIT LUGD. BAT. 10 DEC. 1891.

JOHANNES HENDRICUS CASPARUS KERN

E PAGO POERWOREDJO (JAVA). NATUS 6 APR. 1833.
PROF. IN COLL. REGIN. BENARES. 1863. LING. SANSKRIT.
PROF. ORD. IN UNIV. LUGD. BAT. 18 OCT. 1865.
EMER. 1903. OBIIT ULTR. TRA.. 4 JUL. 1917.

3

Unity and Plurality

LEIDEN
UNIVERSITY

1975 - TODAY

A Happy Medium

If there was one thing that the new Netherlands of the last few decades lacked, it was its old gift for seeking out the centre ground. The country's wealth, strangely enough, was to blame. With this prosperity had grown a sanguine belief that the Netherlands and its people were self-made products. This idea subsequently forked into two mutually antagonistic branches: the levelling out of differences and individualisation. The former spawned a long series of government measures designed to ensure that all Dutch citizens shared equally in the country's wealth. The latter led to the dismantling of pillarisation, the arrangement that had kept the Netherlands together for so long. The levelling out principle led to a concentrated drive to spread knowledge and to redistribute power and income, while individualisation abolished the old function of churches and political parties, leading to a polarisation in public debate.

The Netherlands thus adopted an expensive ideology of equality just when the oil crisis was turning a budgetary surplus into a dramatic deficit. Suddenly the country was in trouble, without the traditional pillars that had once been its mainstay. The process of recovery, an operation comparable to the Delta works built after the dramatic floods of 1953, resulted in the polder model, yielding a consensus not just between employers and employees, but across the entire political spectrum. This model proved so successful that it

numbed the general public's urge to debate fundamental issues; the Dutch happily allowed external forces to dictate their fate. But an uneasy sense gradually took hold that their country was slipping out of their control. It was being refashioned by an assertive outside world, through an elaborate web of European Union legislation and burgeoning ethnic minorities that seemed disinclined to take part in Dutch culture. Two political assassinations later (of the politician Pim Fortuyn and the film-maker Theo van Gogh), the country recovered its sense of what mattered: that permanent quest for the happy medium between extremes.

The Fourth Centenary

In 1975, Leiden University too pondered the question of its identity as it prepared to celebrate its fourth centenary. Unlike the university's founding ceremony, the commemorations did not start with a church service; nor were they held early in the morning or in the middle of winter. It must be said that the opening of the festivities, on the steps of the town hall, was a distinctly unimaginative occasion. As a symbolic gesture, the university keys – mansized, green wooden things – were presented to the mayor, whose speech of thanks was drowned by the chimes from the nearby church. A rather awkward silence ensued, into which ventured the president of the university's executive board, K.J. Cath, to declare that the university was 'more open than in the past'.

'Openness' was certainly the impression that the university strained to create, that May week. While the sun rolled over the roofs and all the carnivalesque accessories that had been squirreled away in cupboards were brought out to play, the celebrations also served a serious purpose: an exhibition of all that the university had to offer. The festivities presented the perfect opportunity, the president of the board had said, opening the academic year, 'to show the outside world what the university has done and is doing with its freedom, and how the university, as a goal-oriented community, can contribute to the development of society.' He described the predicament of an

◄ *University administration building, former University Library*

institution that had been 'put on the defensive'. The university's poor public image, the steady growth in the number of students and their widely differing motives for studying, the institution's burgeoning list of tasks and its shrinking resources, the tension between responsibilities and administrative structure, and between teaching and research, it all created a worrying litany as an overture to the centennial celebrations.

The festive week itself, crammed with a dizzying programme of activities, had two basic aims. The first was to introduce the university to the city and the country at large, bringing it out of its ivory tower and holding open house. This led to all sorts of merry activities with sports and games, music and drama, and a great deal more besides: market stalls and puppet shows, strength sports and folk dancing, numerous distressed children who had lost their parents in the crowds, odd-looking clothes (costumes from Volendam and Tirol), grease stains and belly-aches, blisters, and rousing renditions of *'Io Vivat'*. The relay race courses along the streets were chalked so boldly that motorists used them as parking spaces the next day.

The second goal was to see whether the university was living up to its motto, *'Praesidium Libertatis'* (Bastion of Liberty). Specific disciplines and the general idea-forming process within the academic community were screened for the presence of social or scholarly constraints. An impressive 82 institutions held open house in this connection. Books, exhibitions, symposiums and conferences were on offer in all shapes and sizes. The main attractions were the big symposiums organised by the law and social sciences faculty. The lawyers passionately debated the theme of 'law and the freedom of the individual', with the Baader-Meinhof trial a divisive, polarising background presence. The sociologists tackled the theme, 'dependency, independence, freedom, in relation to colonisation and decolonisation'. Here, the so-called decolonisation model of Vietnam and Cambodia/China provoked a crackling debate.

The most traditional, and most important, part of the centenary week was an academic session in which 14 scholars from three continents were awarded honorary doctorates, before an assembly that included representatives of 32 universities from 21 countries in addition to the Queen and the Crown

▲ *Tower of the main university building on Rapenburg canal*

Princess and their consorts. The hundred-strong cortège of professors from the main university building to St Peter's Church, wearing garments no less colourful than those of a Balinese funeral and accompanied by strains from Valerius's *Gedenck-Clanck*, was in itself an overwhelming scene. The fourteen new honorary doctors, eleven of whom attended the ceremony, were all renowned scholars: they included Emmanuel Levinas and François Braudel.

In A.E. Cohen's rector's speech at the beginning of the ceremony, A.E. Cohen renounced all the superlatives with which his predecessor had distinguished Leiden from the Netherlands' other universities. The only one he wished to retain was that of being the oldest. The theme of this centenary speech was the disintegration of the institution that the university had once been, since 'the mutual differences between our faculties and branches of study, the distinction between our departments and administrative layers have combined to give our universities the appearance of complete heterogeneity.'

Cohen argued that a scholar's commitment to his special subject was many times greater than that to his university. This led him to predict the disintegration of the individual institution and the genesis of a 'Universitas Neerlandica'. More enduring than the institution as such, he hoped, would be the spirit that had inspired its sixteenth-century founders: 'the civic virtues of respect, style, dignity and tolerance'. In his closing words he added another virtue, 'salutary doubt ... the root of all knowledge'.

The differences between the academy of 1575 and the university of 1975 are certainly very striking. One had nothing to lose and only a future, the other had everything to lose and was suffused with a sense of its past. Any comparison between the university of 1575 and that of 1975, between rebellious province and established kingdom, between besieged city and languid municipality, between the fresh new educational establishment and its four-centuries-old descendant, is bound to be untenable. Still, the comparison does demonstrate that in 1975, Leiden University was plunged into a mood of unprecedented self-doubt.

◄ *Procession held to mark the 2008 anniversary of the university's foundation day, with the beadle, rector magnificus and the* Dies *lecturer*

Scandals

This challenge was aggravated three times in the 1990s by scandals that generated considerable internal unrest and badly damaged the university's reputation. Two celebrated professors were compelled to resign, and the president of the executive board saw his impressive career come to an ignominious end. The professors' resignations paired personal tragedy to turmoil within their faculties, while that of the president shook the university's very foundations. All three were dramatic events, not least because of the prominent role played by hubris and blindness.

The first of these affairs, involving the criminologist Buikhuisen, was a pure product of the *Zeitgeist*, a natural consequence of the fervent commitment to social progress that marked the 1980s. Buikhuisen was the director of the Research and Documentation Centre for Policy Research at the Ministry of Justice. When he was appointed to a chair in Leiden, in 1978, the monthly probation and aftercare journal *KRI* reported that Buikhuisen was planning to study the brains of delinquents. That was not in fact the case. Buikuizen wanted to research 'the interaction between biological and social factors' in criminal behaviour, to correct what he saw as a one-sided emphasis on social factors. He did not have any intention either of conducting brain research or of using detainees as experimental subjects. Even so, his 'secret plans' immediately became front-page news, and he was soon being vilified as a latter-day Lombroso.

In retrospect, this reaction is hardly surprising, coming as it did at a time when the film *One flew over de cuckoo's nest* was filling auditoria and the CIA was being blamed for all the world's problems. In Leiden, the general consensus was initially to ignore the media fuss. Even the one-man guerrilla launched against Buikhuisen by Hugo Brandt Corstius, one of the country's most gifted polemicists, did not jeopardise Buikhuisen's position; Brandt Corstius made it perfectly clear that he was engaging in literary polemic, and intended his words to be read in that spirit. That less well-appointed minds took his comments literally and posted boxes of excrement to the professor's home was a woeful corollary.

▶ *Wall poem on the rear façade of the university administration building at Rapenburg 70*

STOA

Wie de slag van 't zwemmen en de kunst
Zich door golven te doen dragen leerde
Kreunt zich langer om ongunst noch gunst
Van 't getijde. 't Onvermijdbre zinken
Beangst hem niet. Het bitterste te drinken
Is aan 't eind misschien het dan begeerde.

ALBERT VERWEY (1865-1937)

The problem was that Buikhuisen had neither social intelligence nor a capacity for theoretical nuance. Profoundly convinced of the value of his research and an *Einzelgänger* by nature, he responded poorly to criticism and rebutted it bluntly. He ended up alienating not only fellow-criminologists and his faculty, but also those who had worked alongside him, legal scholars and social scientists alike. Well-founded criticism of his proposals was submitted, most notably from the social sciences faculty. Data theorists were astonished by the 'monumental vagueness' of his plans, while jurists criticised his inability to identify the relationships between scientific and moral categories. The net result was to plunge a study explicitly designed as interdisciplinary into

▲ *Address given by the biologist Edward Wilson in the senate chamber of the main university building*

complete isolation. This, combined with the unrelenting opposition and anonymous allegations that plagued him, made Buikhuisen decide in 1989 to abandon university life and become an antiquarian. That research of this kind is conducted everywhere nowadays, and that biology is accorded a key place in legal studies as well as in social science research, highlights the true proportions of this tragic case.

The second major scandal related to the university's management of its own property. An obscure contract that the director of operational management awarded a company to build an annex to the Sylvius laboratory prompted an enquiry that laid low the President of the Executive Board, C.P.C.M. Oomen. Like the previous case, the transformation of a molehill into a mountainous controversy was a tragedy of character and circumstance.

Oomen was a Leiden-educated legal scholar who had become faculty dean shortly after acquiring his first position as senior lecturer and who had later risen to director-general at the Ministry of Water Management. Though an excellent jurist and an effective administrator, he was not lacking in a certain hubris. From the outset he made no bones about his disdain for the university council: serious decisions had to be made, and he had no time for drivel about organic coffee. He had a physical aversion to the combination of financial prudence and endless cycles of meetings over which he presided. This would prove his Achilles heel in the annex affair.

The annex had originally been conceived as a way of combining speed with efficiency. The end result was the exact opposite. The structure, intended for preclinical research, would be built by Fibomij, a financing company created especially for the purpose. The problem was that the estate agent who had founded Fibomij, who had never built anything in his life, enlisted the services of a building company whose director turned out to have a history of bankruptcies, who in turn hired a contractor with a tradition of lagging behind or defaulting on payments. In these conditions, the project initially resembled a comedy more than a tragedy. Directors came and went as in a game of musical chairs, the builders were more often absent than at work, the tax inspectorate and public prosecutions department raided the financing company and building company, and to cap it all, the university's director of operational management, who bore direct responsibility for the project, appeared to be so deeply implicated that he was suspected of involvement with a criminal organisation.

Until then, the executive board and university council had cooperated amicably in Leiden's 'harmony model'. This model, based on shared responsibility and a willingness to compromise, was showing signs of wear. More importantly, however, Oomen was not the right man to sustain it, partly because he neglected to maintain the crucial close ties with the faculty deans. So as the council fumed at its powerlessness and the deans maintained a studious neutrality, Oomen, as the holder of the building portfolio, was held responsible for a serious error on the part of one of his senior officials. The stage was set for a miniature history play.

The same epithet was used to describe the plagiarism scandal that compelled the clinical psychologist René Diekstra to resign in 1996. The magnitude of this affair can be gauged by the fact that he was the first professor in the Netherlands ever to resign for such a reason, and that he was a highly successful scholar. Diekstra had been appointed professor of clinical and health psychology in 1979, at 33 years of age. He was a much-loved teacher and a prolific author of books, articles and columns; he combined his professorship with important advisory positions, besides editing six journals and running a private practice as a psychotherapist.

In this latter activity, he did not confine himself to individual clients; he happily turned his clinical gaze on the Dutch population as a whole. In the 1980s, he had become a successful purveyor of popular science in newspaper columns, articles and books of essays with titles like *Je verdriet voorbij* ('On the other side of sadness') *Pleisters voor de ziel* ('Plasters for your soul') and *Als het leven pijn doet* ('When living hurts'). These books were based on the idea 'that we are all the keepers of our brothers and sisters'. Diekstra's role in popular science peaked when he was given his own TV programme, '*Het onderste boven*' ('Upside down'). The book of the same title that was published after the series ended would trigger his fall.

After the weekly magazine *Vrij Nederland* revealed that 15 pages of 'Upside down' had simply been lifted from another self-help book, it was soon

▲ *Former home of Professor Christiaan Snouck Hurgronje (1857-1936), now Leiden University Fund*

discovered that in other publications too, Diekstra had frequently copied long passages from other people's books, sometimes including very brief references and sometimes failing to do even that. Diekstra's defence – the pressure of time, poor editing – was weak, and was undermined by reports of a case of plagiarism in a scientific publication. The case assumed biblical proportions when it transpired that one of the whistle-blowers was one of Diekstra's own students. A committee appointed especially to investigate the matter concluded that Diekstra's popularising books could not be separated from his professorial responsibilities, and that they should meet the same standards. The executive board endorsed the committee's report, and after parting company with its 'latter-day Lombroso', Leiden had to bid farewell to its 'cheating professor'.

That was by no means the end of the matter. Aside from the passionate support of many of his students, who set up the Committee to Assist René to the End (CARE) ('Stop the press, burn *Vrij Nederland*'), he also received support of academics who felt strongly that popular science *should* be distinguished from academic work, who wanted Diekstra's accusers to prove that the ill-fated professor had deliberately set out to claim the glory due to others, and who concluded that what was at stake was a copyright issue rather than a case of plagiarism. Anyone who compares the opposing opinions is forced to conclude that the debate about plagiarism was drowned by the deafening roar of vanity and fall.

Legislation

In the three decades of education policy that have elapsed since the 1970s, three phases can be distinguished, with the 1980s as the turning-point and the change from regulation to deregulation as the most important theme. To put it in political terms, the socialist 1970s made way for the Christian Democrat 1980s, which were, in turn, succeeded by the liberal (largely in the sense of economically laissez-faire) 1990s. It should be added that the political colour of policy was not the only motor of change; economic conditions and the willingness of decision-makers to allow policy to be guided by social trends were also highly influential.

The 1970 University Administration (Reform) Act (WUB) introduced joint decision-making powers for all staff and students at every level. It was this, more than the openness and public nature of administration, that encountered considerable opposition from administrators and professors – so much so, in fact, that rectors such as Cohen and Beenakker defined their administrative mission largely in terms of damage limitation in the wake of the new legislation. Combined with external democratisation – 'all those who apply and are suitable must in principle be admitted' – the Act created two kinds of tension: between democracy and effective administration and between expansion and funding.

The combination of an explosive rise in university student numbers and the need for government cutbacks led to proposals for two sweeping changes: shorter courses, to be divided into stages, and a new division of responsibilities, concentrating disciplines within specific institutions. The question was who should take the initiative. Where the task allocation and concentration operation was concerned, two alternatives were proposed: a platform of national advisors from the faculties or each university's development of its own specific profile. The first solution would effectively abolish the universities, while the second would emphasise their autonomy and identity. In the end, it was decided to define specific profiles, to eliminate weaknesses and highlight strengths, not through consultation but American-style, through competition.

As for altering the length of courses, the universities opted for a two-stage period of study, which was adapted after a few years to the Anglo-Saxon system of bachelor's and master's degrees. The decision to adopt a four-year period of study brought other developments in its train which had their roots in the United States, such as the modular structure of each individual's course of study, the introduction of a credit system, and the possibility of swapping credits with those issued by other institutions providing higher education.

In the 1990s, the universities recognised that autonomy would improve their ability to attune teaching and research to developments in society and to

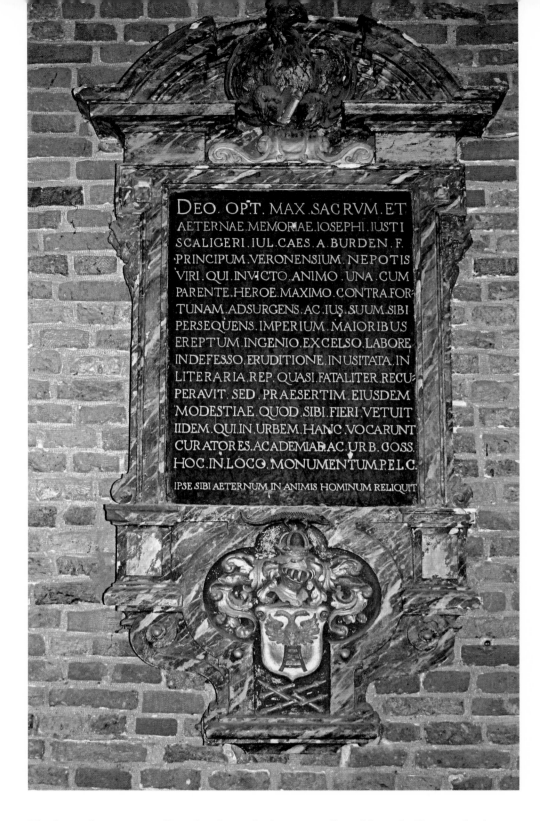

DEO. OPT. MAX. SACRVM. ET.
AETERNAE. MEMORIAE. IOSEPHI. IVSTI
SCALIGERI. IVL. CAES. A. BVRDEN. F.
PRINCIPVM. VERONENSIVM. NEPOTIS
VIRI. QVI. INVICTO. ANIMO. VNA. CVM
PARENTE. HEROE. MAXIMO. CONTRA. FOR-
TVNAM. ADSVRGENS. AC. IVS. SVVM. SIBI
PERSEQVENS. IMPERIVM. MAIORIBVS
EREPTVM. INGENIO. EXCELSO. LABORE
INDEFESSO. ERVDITIONE. INVSITATA. IN
LITERARIA. REP. QVASI. FATALITER. RECV-
PERAVIT. SED. PRAESERTIM. EIVSDEM
MODESTIAE. QVOD. SIBI. FIERI. VETVIT
IIDEM. QVI. IN. VRBEM. HANC. VOCARVNT
CVRATORES. ACADEMIAE. AC. VRB. COSS.
HOC. IN. LOCO. MONVMENTVM. P. E. L. C.

IPSE. SIBI. AETERNVM. IN. ANIMIS. HOMINVM. RELIQVIT

▲   *The funeral monument of Josephus Justus Scaliger, transferred from the Vrouwenkerk
to St Peter's Church*

HIER LEIT BEGRAVEN MR LUDOLPH VAN CEULEN
GEWESEN NEDERDUYTSCH PROFESSOR INDE
WIS@NSTIGE WETENSCHAPPEN INDE HOGE
SCHOLE DESER STEDE GEBOREN IN HILDESHEIM
INT JAER 1540 DEN XXVIII JANUARY ENDE GE
STORVEN DEN XXXI DECEMBER 1610 DE WELCKE
IN SYN LEVEN DOOR VEEL ARBEYDS DES RONDS
OMLOOPS NAESTE REDEN TEGEN SYN MIDDEL
LYN GEVONDEN HEEFT ALS HIER VOLCHT

ALS
DE MIDDELLYN IS
I
DAN IS DEN OMLOOP MEERDER ALS

$$3\frac{14159265358979323846264338327950288}{10000000000000000000000000000000000000}$$

EN MINDER ALS

$$3\frac{14159265358979323846264338327950289}{10000000000000000000000000000000000000}$$

MAER ALS DE MIDDELLYN IS

DAN IS DEN OMLOOP MEERDER ALS 31415926535897932384...

EN MINDERALS 31415926535897932384626433832795028...

GEPLAATST DOOR HET WISKUNDIG GENOOTSCHAP 5 JULI 2000
EEN ONVERMOEIDE ARBEID KOMT ALLES TE BOVEN

▲ *Funeral monument of Ludolf van Ceulen, lector in applied mathematics and fencing master*

changes in market conditions. The University Government (Modernisation) Act (MUB, 1997) gave each university a supervisory board and endowed the executive boards with sweeping powers. At faculty level, the dean acquired greater powers, while at the lowest administrative level, a director of studies (*opleidingsdirecteur*) could be appointed. Universities acquired far more say than in the past regarding the way they structured the various courses on offer. The quality of teaching and research was monitored in regular inspections by specially appointed experts.

As for funding, the old model, based on statements of expenses, was changed into a mix of input and output norms. The education part of the fixed resources is now distributed among universities on the basis of student registrations and numbers graduating. Tuition fees were paid directly to the universities themselves. The amount of these fees is currently set by central government, but there is a lively debate going on about allowing universities to set their own fees. The research part of the resources is divided into four components: basic facilities, special provision for Ph.D. students, research institutes, and strategic concerns.

While for years the emphasis was on increasing student numbers, in the 1990s the accent shifted to quality. Financial controllability constrained university admissions, and grants were used to encourage students to progress more quickly (new terms such as 'speed grant' and 'achievement grant' entered the language). Universities were also authorised to issue binding recommendations to students at the end of their first year.

Another major innovation was the development of explicit policy on university research from the 1980s onwards. The Policy Document on University Research (BUOZ, 1979) made a start on plans for research programming, prioritisation and so forth. Annual research reports were introduced in 1979, followed by the conditional funding of research in 1982. In addition, the mid-1990s saw the gradual acceptance of the belief that university research needed a more dynamic thrust, to increase its support within society at large. To achieve this, the government strengthened the second flow of funds, through the Netherlands Organisation for Scientific Research (NWO).

► *Wall poem by Christophe Plantijn*

SONNET.
LE BONHEUR
DE CE MONDE.

Avoir une maifon commode, propre & belle,
Un jardin tapiffé d'efpaliers odorans,
Des fruits, d'excellent vin, peu de train, peu d'enfans,
Poffeder feul, fans bruit, une femme fidéle.

N'avoir dettes, amour, ni procés, ni querelle,
Ni de partage à faire avecque fes parens,
Se contenter de peu, n'efpérer rien des Grands,
Régler tous fes deffeins fur un jufte modéle.

Vivre avecque franchife & fans ambition,
S'adonner fans fcrupule à la dévotion,
Domter fes paffions, les rendre obéiffantes.

Conferver l'efprit libre, & le jugement fort,
Dire fon Chapelet en cultivant fes entes,
C'eft attendre chez foi bien doucement la mort.

CHRISTOPHLE PLANTIN (ca 1520 -1589)

Administration

The most important decisions to be made, at a university as elsewhere, relate to appointments, and the most important appointment of all is the chair of the executive board. Five men held this post at Leiden University in the period 1972-2006. All were good administrators, but they had very different personalities. And just as a Renaissance reign was shaped by the monarch's *virtus*, the personality of the chair of the executive board determined the difference between success and failure, leadership and kismet. In retrospect, Leiden's liberal university can be said to have gone through a Leninist pattern of change: two steps forwards and one back.

The first chairman, K.J. Cath (1972-1988), remained in office longer than any other. He succeeded in transforming the polarised relations that had dominated the first board operating within the framework of the University Administration (Reform) Act (WUB) into an effective 'harmony model' and in shifting the focus of debate from ideological exchanges on the nature of a university to more pragmatic issues. Cath was a legal scholar with wide-ranging experience. Highly active in student life during and after the war, he had later spent several years working in commerce. This background, combined with his Frisian temperament and infectious sense of humour, helped him to effect a gradual transition from aristocratic administration to modern management.

The main difficulty lay in forging constructive working relationships between the university council and the executive board, and between these two bodies and the faculties. The first of these relationships was complicated by clashing areas of competence. The council dealt in general principles, while the executive board was responsible for the day-to-day preparation and implementation of policy. By involving the council in its work, and by inviting the chairs of the various council committees to attend its meetings, the board could forestall disputes about competence. The relations between the administrative bodies and the faculties were strained because of the government's refusal to match the growing demand for education with a proportionate increase in staff. The pressure this brought to bear on expensive forms of

◄ *Former pharmaceutical laboratory, now Horizon House of Leiden Student Housing Bureau*

education and research was soon translated into an atmosphere of mutual rivalry. To solve this problem, a new system of multi-annual agreements was introduced, based on education and research capacity in each course of study – backed up by well-reasoned arguments – which made it possible to avoid ideological debates in this area too. Every faculty could now define its own specific profile, yielding a well-founded and negotiable package of responsibilities for which it would be given financial protection for a set period of time.

This did mean, however, that the executive and faculty boards had to closely align their administrative activities; in fact it led to a far-reaching integration of their powers. And this in turn meant that the university council lost its grip on policy and slid back into its old habits of ideological debate. But by then, times had changed. When Cath proposed limiting the council's powers to an advisory role, the proposal provoked a motion against him and a protracted evening debate. But the motion was rejected, and the change later became law.

Cath carried the day in other respects, too. Two points are particularly worth mentioning here. First, he advocated a more efficient way of running the university, culminating in a presidential system, and second, it was he who urged that quality should be the sole significant criterion in determining the profile of Leiden University. Interestingly, both these factors presupposed greater autonomy and a far greater distance from government, a construction that had been a bridge too far for the university of 1900 and that was now simply imposed on it.

Cath's successor was Oomen, and the scandal that led to his resignation would have severe repercussions. From then on, university property – not just in Leiden – would be administered more professionally. This much-publicised scandal was also clearly one of the factors underlying the minister's decision, with the introduction of the University Government (Modernisation) Act (MUB, 1997), to furnish every university or college of higher professional education with its own supervisory board. In board members such as Hazelhoff from De Nederlandsche Bank and Tabaksblat from Unilever, Leiden University acquired heavyweights from the business world. Faculty

deans were also given more influence. In many cases, especially for the larger faculties, professional administrators were recruited.

The new board chairman who would be responsible for steering these changes through smoothly was Loek Vredevoogd, a man initially recruited as an interim manager to defuse the existing crisis. Vredevoogd lived up to his name – which translates into Dutch as 'Guardian of the Peace'. He had studied not at Leiden but at the Vrij Universiteit (Free University) of Amsterdam, and had pursued a career as a civil servant at the education ministry before being appointed chair of the executive board of the Open University. Yet he had a finely-tuned sense of the atmosphere in Leiden, and decided to strike while the iron was hot. What is more, that iron – Vredevoogd had a touch of the King Midas about him without the unfortunate side-effects – soon turned out to be gold.

▲ *The Gravensteen, former legal studies centre, now International Office and Leiden University School of Management*

▲ *Former Kamerlingh Onnes Laboratory, now legal studies centre*
▼ *Library of the legal studies centre*

Vredevoogd was a past master in building broad support for measures that were all in fact designed with only one purpose in mind: to make Leiden into a top university. Under his leadership, the Committee of Deans came to work in close collaboration with the executive board. In addition, so-called 'strategic conferences' were held from 1997 onwards. From its first major strategic plan onwards, the 1994 policy document 'Koersen op Kwaliteit' (Steering by Quality), Leiden University again succeeded in refashioning a profile for itself, which might be called (by analogy to the *philosophia novantiqua*) an ancient-modern synthesis. This process appeared set to continue under Vredevoogd's successor, Anne Willem Kist, but a lack of affinity with the university led Kist to resign after only two years in office. For Leiden, this was another retrograde step.

Through all these ins and sometimes painful outs, the university was fortunate enough to have a series of rectors who combined an ability to focus on specific problem areas with dedicated commitment. After the long rectorship of Dolf Cohen (1972-1976), 'a wise man if ever there was one', the university acquired in the environmental biologist Donald Kuenen someone whose great sense of humour and understatement stood him in good stead as he guided the university through the turbulent events of the late 1970s. The clinical chemist Kassenaar (1979-1985) was a man cut from a very different mould. He had a penchant for operating in the superlative by invoking the Holy Trinity, but he was exceedingly effective in what was later called, in a clumsy turn of phrase, the 'valorisation' of research or the transfer of knowledge, through ties with industry.

Kassenaar was the first in a series of rectors who developed clear-cut ideas on education policy. His own main concerns were to preserve the cohesiveness of education and research and to promote research institutes. The same applied to his successor, the experimentalist physicist Beenakker (1985-1991). Every inch a researcher – Beenakker admitted that he felt jealous if he heard his son and colleague talking about his research – he did not see his administrative duties as a visionary mission. 'You can never see past the next bend in the river,' he used to say.

His successor, the theologian Leertouwer (1991-1997), was a very different kind of man, more scholar than researcher, an effective public speaker, perhaps in part precisely because of his faltering speech. Leertouwer was also a skilled, experienced administrator who had worked with everything from trade unions to the media. He would dedicate himself wholeheartedly to the language and literature of the 'minor languages' (that is, those with relatively few students) and teacher training, besides promoting opportunities for students to occupy administrative positions through 'administration grants'. In time he developed into a real education rector, advocating intake interviews with applicant students and keenly endorsing the proposals of the report 'Steering by Quality', such as the possibility of issuing students with binding recommendations and more especially the introduction of closer supervision.

His successor, the psychologist Wagenaar (1997-2001), a man with artistic leanings like Leertouwer, with a passion for home play readings and pop-up books, also liked to operate at the interface of education and research. In the social science faculty he had devised a system for verifying and comparing research, and as rector he sought to introduce similar controls to monitor the quality of teaching. In contrast to Leertouwer, a farmer's son who looked ill at ease in a suit, Wagenaar sported a bow tie and carefully trimmed moustache, but he too was a 'teaching rector', who floated a number of ideas – better pay for good teachers, compulsory teaching experience as part of a master's degree course, credits for sports – that were designed to create a more cheerful atmosphere in Leiden. It was his firm support for binding recommendations that helped this proposal to take root.

Then Leiden acquired another farmer's son, the pharmacologist Breimer from Friesland. One of the university's most celebrated scientists, with a unique blend of charm and authority, he made his mark on virtually every area of university administration. Sweeping reorganisations within faculties, difficult changes such as the introduction of the bachelor-master system, improved student housing and facilities, closer ties with industry, securing an international orientation through the League of European Research Universities, they all benefited crucially from Breimer's great standing within the university. He was in fact the ideal person to introduce the presidential model, the combination of rectorship and chair of the executive board, devised after the disappointing experience with Kist. His departure from the university in 2007 had overtones of a minor deification.

Profile

That the debate on university profiles was imposed from the outside can easily be inferred from the text of the new higher education legislation. It was the enforced division of responsibilities, above all, that compelled universities to decide which subjects they wanted to concentrate on. Initially, these choices related largely to teaching, and solutions were sought by highlighting their relevance to society and devising interdisciplinary education programmes. Later, the advent of conditional funding unleashed passionate debates on the redistribution of the money available to fund research.

Funding remained a pivotal issue. Just when Leiden had opted for a mission geared towards excellence, in its 1987-1991 Development Plan, it found itself confronted with declining student numbers and consequently shrinking resources. Even so, the Leiden debate on profiles constantly revolved around ways of reducing volume and increasing quality, and around the specific ratio of teaching to research. Initially, the university's only response was to veer back and forth, emphasising research at the expense of education until financial estimates necessitated a radical swing in the opposite direction.

Although this was a crucial debate, mapping out the general contours within which conclusions would eventually crystallise, the real turning-point came with the executive board's first strategic plan, 'Steering by Quality', published in 1994 under the chairmanship of Loek Vredevoogd. This policy document also marked the beginning of a truly radical decision-making process, which not only set the university's new course, but defined a series of principles that chimed remarkably well with its historical past. Foremost among them was the firm belief that several false dogmas of equality dating from the 1970s would have to be jettisoned in favour of a new climate of change and flexibility. To aim for quality was to embrace differentiation and selec-

▶ *Former outpatient clinic for internal medicine, now Pieter de la Court building of the Faculty of Social Sciences*
▶▶ *Stairwell in the Pieter de la Court building*

tion in education and research, in personnel policy and financial management.

Perhaps the most important feature of this plan was not so much its insistence on quality as its detailed proposals for improving *teaching*. In part, this emphasis was undoubtedly inspired by Leiden's loss of an alarmingly large proportion of the education market and the crucial importance of student numbers, if only as a source of funding. But it was also an emphasis that guaranteed widespread support for the plan within the university.

Starting from the premise of academic education – that is, education closely entwined with research – several key proposals were made to improve the quality of teaching: issuing binding recommendations to students after their foundation course results, intensifying ties between staff and students, structuring the curriculum carefully within each discipline, and paying close attention to didactic qualities when selecting academic staff. To safeguard the breadth of each course, the curriculum would include a general, inter-faculty component – a revised general studies course – besides which the role of student clubs and societies would be reinforced. In the master's phase, education would be geared primarily to identifying outstanding students and creating facilities such as high-quality tutorials, master-classes and foreign exchange programmes.

In research, the main emphasis was on formulating profile-defining research programmes at faculty and inter-faculty level, limiting the number of focal areas and introducing internal quality control. Other innovations included more flexible personnel and pay policies, wider professorial mandates, part-time appointments, rejuvenating the staff, and attracting up-and-coming talent by creating places for research assistants and postdoctoral researchers.

Subsequent plans (University Strategies I and II or 'Wegen naar gehalte' 1999/2000, and Focusing on Talent or 'Kiezen voor Talent', 2005) further elaborated and modified this profile. University Strategies mainly highlighted Leiden's specific 'educational environment', besides focusing on issues like quality control, internationalisation and ICT. The plans it presented were dominated by the need to introduce Bachelor's and Master's degrees and the opportunities that would accompany this system. Where teaching was con-

cerned, the link with research and the discipline-based structure continued to feature prominently, but besides maximising academic skills the plan also emphasised preparation for professional careers and challenged faculties to create new courses with this aim in mind. Examples include 'Entrepreneurship, Law and Management' and 'Humanities in practice'.

The creativity of this period yielded two new institutes. First, in 1999 Leiden joined forces with Delft University of Technology to form the 'Hague Campus'. Initially a platform for lectures, it soon spawned two regular evening courses, in law and political science. In 2002 the new institute acquired a third course in Public Affairs, operating at the interface of industry, government and civic society. The Arts Faculty founded in 2001, a joint initiative of the university and the Royal Academy of Fine Arts, Design, Music and Dance, besides offering opportunities to students with multiple talents, would also enrich education and research at the fascinating interface of art and science.

▲ *Entrance to the Gorlaeus Laboratory*

The university's 2005 plan 'Focusing on Talent' incorporated the above ideas, but channelled them largely in the direction of a research university, Leiden's self-definition at the outset of the profiles debate. Expanding research focal areas and setting up research consortia were the main principles underlying this policy document, which adopted a more international perspective than earlier plans. Like its predecessors, however, it included proposals to improve teaching, broaching new initiatives such as a Pre-University College for gifted secondary-school pupils, widening the bachelor's phase by dividing it into major and minor subjects, and improving facilities for students. The main emphasis, however, was on the structure of graduate schools and on international recruitment for the postgraduate phase. Leiden consolidated its identity as a research university.

Infrastructure

The centrifugal forces to which a modern university is exposed are obvious from the spaces they occupy within the urban environment: that is, many different premises, frequently far apart. In Leiden there are three. First and foremost, there is the Rapenburg complex, the university's beginning and its centre. That was the original site of the main university building and its botanical gardens, library and anatomy theatre, it was where the professors lived. The Rapenburg was known in the seventeenth century as 'the realm of Pallas'. Well into the nineteenth century, when the authority of Latin had ebbed away, it remained Leiden's *quartier latin*. The university's sphere of influence did not expand through the city until the advent of the various teaching hospitals and the laboratories at Vreewijk.

It took some time for the building activities to resume after the Second World War. In the early 1950s, the Kamerlingh Onnes Laboratory acquired a new wing and the Gravensteen building was converted into a legal studies centre. The biology laboratories on the Kaiserstraat and the new clinic for internal medicine date from the late 1950s.

After the war, two new locations opened for teaching and research, one on

◄ *Huygens Laboratory (left) and Gorlaeus Laboratory (right) in the Leeuwenhoek*

Witte Singel and the other in the Leeuwenhoek complex. The latter acquired, next to the academic hospital, a series of laboratories and the Social Science Institute (formerly the outpatient clinic for internal medicine). The Witte Singel site was earmarked for a new library and the humanities (including theology). This meant that Leiden University had railway lines running straight through it. Passengers heading for the exact or social sciences left from the west exit of Central Station, while those wanting the humanities left from the east exit.

In 1957 the municipal authorities of Leiden and Oegstgeest drafted a joint structural plan granting the university about a hundred hectares of polder land between Central Station and the A 44 highway. Since the new rectangular site was destined for the medicine, mathematics and physics faculties, it was named after Antonie van Leeuwenhoek. The initial, audacious, plan envisaged an American-style campus: a central building with general facilities and a large lecture-hall on a raised plateau, over an underground car park. A broad flight of steps would connect the plateau to a central passageway, with a circular walkway some six metres above ground level providing access to six laboratory towers.

The final result would be very different. Following the Wassenaarseweg, the first building one comes to, no. 64, is the Clusius biochemistry laboratory. In the 1980s this laboratory moved to the Gorlaeus building and made way for the Institute of Molecular Botany. No. 72 was the Sylvius laboratory, two adjacent nine-story tower blocks for medical and biological research and teaching. A little further on, with its entrance on Einsteinweg, stands the Gorlaeus complex, a towering cube of a building erected in the 1960s, attached to a spectacular saucer-shaped lecture-hall and a large, almost transparent laboratory for undergraduates (the LMUY).

The second tower block consists of the Huygens Laboratory and the Snellius, both from the 1970s. The Snellius building houses the computing centre and the Institute of Advanced Computer Science (LIACS). Far more recent and therefore more fashionable additions are the slanting J.H. Oort building and the vibration-free Kamerlingh Onnes 'measurement hall'. The Bio-Science Park was built around the Gorlaeus-Huygens-Oort complex in

▲ *Wall bearing the signatures of those who took part in the Ehrenfest Colloquium, including names such as Bohr, Oppenheimer, Einstein, and Becquerel. Formerly in the Kamerlingh Onnes Laboratory, now in the Oort Building*

the 1980s. The university sports centre had opened in the vicinity in 1970, enabling students to take part in 35 different sports at the centre and elsewhere. Back near central station rise the blue and yellow blocks of the new Academic Hospital, now called Leiden University Medical Centre (LUMC). Its first wing opened in 1985, and the second in 1996. More recent still are the impressive buildings for research and teaching that opened in 2005 and 2007, respectively.

The sharp split between the 'two cultures' embodied by the railway line that divided them might have been more forbidding still if the original plans for Witte Singel, including a 125-metre high tower block, had been implemented. But the tower block met with fierce opposition, and when the Ministry of Defence's catering college moved out of the Doelen complex, there was sufficient space for low-rise buildings on Witte Singel. It was decided to build several clusters, a library flanked by wings for Western languages, theology, philosophy and archaeology to the east of Witte Singel, while to the west there would be buildings for non-Western languages in the Doelen

▲　*Two of three stained-glass windows by the artist Harm Kamerlingh Onnes with a picture of the discovery of the Zeeman effect*

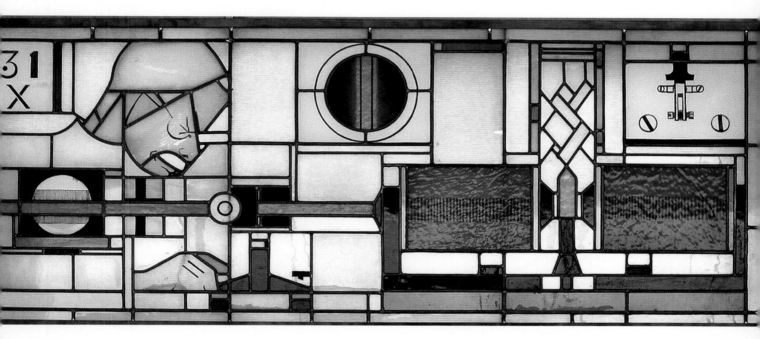

complex (including the restoration of those beside the Doelenpoort), with a
central facilities structure and buildings for history and art history. The latter stand out most notably by not standing out at all, and indeed fit perfectly
into the public housing projects that surround them. The library is reminiscent of a prehistoric reptile flanked by a harem-less Ottoman palace, while
the facilities building looks rather like a grain silo. The library opened in
1984.

   Finally, attention turned back to the Rapenburg. The former library, which
had been providing temporary accommodation for the herbarium for several
years, was finally given a new lease of life in 1999. As the 'old university library', it has become the university's administrative centre. Since the 1960s,
the executive board and offices of the university had been encamped in the
ugliest (and draughtiest) building imaginable, Stationsweg 46, right at the dividing line between the two academic cultures, but most conspicuously a
utilitarian eyesore that extinguished any hint of imagination. Through a
combination of tasteful restoration and bright modernisation, the little old

church and structures dating from the nineteenth and early twentieth centuries were forged into a unified whole exuding *Bildung* and thoughtful deliberation, epitomized by the early eighteenth-century ceiling painting of the central meeting-room with the four seasons.

This move was one of several expressions of a totally new way of thinking about the university's architectural image. According to this new approach, the Rapenburg canal was to be the university's defining location. The notion of Rapenburg as the heart of the modern university had been formulated many decades earlier – in 1927 – by Van Vollenhoven. He saw the purchase of the old Rapenburg buildings as the key objective of Leiden's University Fund, the idea being to transform this ancient canal with its seventeenth- and eighteenth-century mansions into a university campus, where an upper middle-class residential culture could blend seamlessly with university institutionalisation. A related initiative was the founding of Leiden's Faculty Club in 1997-1998, which acquired premises at Rapenburg 6, while the Leiden University Fund moved into Snouck Hurgronje's old house at Rapenburg 61. The university still owns seven buildings on Rapenburg.

Other developments arising from this policy involved the renovation of the botanical gardens and the conversion of the old Kamerlingh Onnes laboratory. Today, the botanical gardens display a wide range of horticulture; in 1990 they even acquired a Japanese garden. The most recent addition is the winter garden built in 2000, a large transparent structure with a sub-tropical greenhouse and a visitors' centre. Plans are afoot to combine the botanical gardens and observatory into an integrated centre incorporating visitors' facilities and an astronomy centre. The building once known as Staten College, which later became a riding stables and later still a student canteen (De Bak) underwent radical renovation, opening in 2004 as Plexus, a modern study centre housing over ten student societies and a range of student facilities. That same year, the law faculty moved into the elegantly restyled Kamerlingh Onnes building.

◄   *Leeuwenhoek Bio-Science Park*

The Faculties

For all the differences between the faculties, in size and structure, in objectives and sex appeal, they were all subject to the pressures of the age. They grew and differentiated as the economy flourished, only to be forced into cutbacks and concentration by a downturn in market conditions. While the faculties followed the natural law of fragmentation, the executive board found itself compelled to follow the human desire for uniformity. The main debate within the faculties was as old as the Dutch state: was the faculty a loose-knit conglomeration of disciplines or a discipline-based entity, an alliance or a federation?

Medicine

The university's medical school, which includes the academic hospital, is not only the largest faculty in budgetary as well as staffing terms, it is also the one with the widest range of responsibilities, since patient care is added to its research and education mandates. This care is a derivative of the other responsibilities, but it does mean that practical applications loom larger in the medical faculty than elsewhere. This led to a split between the preclinical and clinical subjects – that is, between those constituting the strict scientific basis of medicine and those geared towards intervention. In Leiden this split was actually translated into a physical divide, with the entrance to the academic hospital located on the Rijnsburgerweg and that to the preclinical laboratories on the Wassenaarseweg.

In the early 1980s, a clear trend emerged towards bridging the gap between preclinical subjects and clinical practice. Clinical applications were devised for techniques originally developed in fundamental research, and researchers forged ties with medical practitioners from an awareness that the *raison d'être* of their research derived from its future clinical usefulness. Certain subjects started to be presented as linking disciplines. Pathology, bacteriology, virology and parasitology were dubbed 'paraclinical' fields:

while not directly involved in patient care, they nonetheless played a contributory role. Pathologists moved closer to the sickbed, as it were, and a similar development emerged in pharmacology and genetics.

In the latter half of the twentieth century, the medical school deliberately styled itself as a research faculty, with a strong bias towards scientific research, most notably in biomedical science and medical technology. At the same time, this faculty in particular did not shrink from critical scrutiny of the moral aspects of physicians' actions, in response to the advent of radical kinds of intervention. Medical ethics became an independent discipline, and a medical ethics committee was formed at the Academic Hospital – the first of its kind in the Netherlands.

▲   *Entrance to the teaching wing of Leiden University Medical Centre*

▲   *Taxonomic garden in the Botanical Gardens*
▼   *Winter garden in the Botanical Gardens*

Following on from this, the faculty developed a curriculum that sought to integrate scientific knowledge into clinical practice: multidisciplinary education with theme blocks as linking modules. Reflections on medical practice, and input from the social sciences, as well as the introduction of general internships, directed the course strongly towards professional practice. At the other end of the spectrum, a new course in biomedical sciences was launched in 1984, to turn out highly-qualified researchers.

The growth of the faculty from 21 professors in 1950 to over a hundred in 1985 made professional management an imperative. In the early 1960s it was decided to split the faculty into four sections, defined roughly as non-clinical, paraclinical, internal pathology, and surgery and obstetrics. A multi-annual deanship was introduced in 1969. Four managing directors were appointed, who were directly responsible to the university's executive board and had a certain freedom of action in relation to the faculty board. During the major reorganisation in 1983, faculty and hospital made an initial attempt to define their research profiles. In the early 1990s, they focused primarily on immunology and transplants, genetics, quantitative cytology, oncology, haemostasis and thrombosis.

In the meantime, the relationship between faculty and academic hospital was being transformed. In 1969 the hospitals became independent organisations under the education ministry, but the various medical disciplines remained under the control of both the university and the ministry. A proposal was put forward to create a clearer management structure in the form of a University Medical Centre, run jointly by the university, the faculty and the academic hospital. This new construction would eventually be introduced, but not for another 25 years later, in a new hospital, Leiden University Medical Centre (LUMC). Although the change was effected by necessity, in the face of further financial cuts, it was channelled towards a successful conclusion by the expert management of Vredevoogd and the hospital director, the neurologist O.J.S. Buruma.

Since this innovation involved the hospital taking over the faculty from the university, there were very real fears of the university losing contact with the LUMC. This did in fact happen, but only temporarily. In this respect too,

Vredevoogd was right when he said: 'In fact you can observe all over the country that the new university medical centres are weakening universities' administrative influence on medical teaching and research. But at the same time, you can also observe in Leiden the good relations that exist between the LUMC and the other faculties, especially mathematics and natural sciences and social sciences. I expect other close ties to mature in the longer term. I believe in the strength of the academic tradition – which for Leiden University is a tradition stretching back for over 400 years.'

Mathematics and Natural Sciences

The faculty of mathematics and natural sciences has also undergone a dramatic process of reorganisation over the past few decades. One element that did not change was the emphasis on research: although student numbers fell sharply in the 1990s, PhD students retained their protected status. But here too, dwindling student numbers made it imperative to rethink the structure of teaching, prompting several changes: students would henceforth choose to graduate in research, secondary-school teaching or management, they could take a range of optional courses, and master classes were introduced.

This faculty grappled with the problem of the faculty's uniformity versus the diversity and autonomy of its various disciplines. At length it was divided into research institutes, and while it adopted a centralised management structure, it delegated certain administrative powers to the academic directors. Other changes related to the number and nature of the courses offered. In 1983 the faculty lost its pharmaceutics course, and a year later geology was closed down. On the positive side, a course in information science was launched in 1982, and in 1985 the faculty introduced a research course in biopharmaceutical sciences. The botanical gardens and herbarium also belonged to the faculty, although the latter was incorporated into the National Herbarium in 1996; the location did not change, since most of the specimens derived from Leiden. The faculty ended up offering a total of seven full-time

▶ *Old Observatory*

courses: mathematics, information science, physics, chemistry, biology, astronomy and biopharmaceutical sciences.

Mathematics research was divided into algebra and number theory, geometry, analysis, mathematical statistics and mathematical decision theory. The Thomas Stieltjes Institute for Mathematics, a joint operation involving seven institutes with its administrative centre in Leiden, was founded in 1992. The activities of the information science course launched in 1982 were concentrated at Leiden Institute of Advanced Computer Science. New themes were proposed: natural computing, artificial life and evolutionary algorithms, neurocomputing, and high performance computing. Astronomy, which had long been one of Leiden's focal attractions, was closely involved in national and international astronomy networks. The interference of radioastronomy with optical and infrared observations led to fruitful collaboration with the Groningen observatory and English institutes. In 1991, Leiden helped found the European Association for Research in Astronomy, currently a forum in which five major institutes participate. One year later, the Dutch astronomy research institute was founded, acquiring a national mandate in 1998.

The physics department has also traditionally emphasised its international ties. Roughly speaking, three main lines of research may be distinguished: theoretical physics, condensed material at low temperatures, and molecular physics and biophysics. Interdisciplinary structures linking biophysics with chemistry were to culminate in the founding of the Leiden School of Fundamental Research on Living Matter, involving theoretical physicists, biologists, medical graduates and mathematicians as well as the groups already mentioned. In chemistry too, collaborative efforts that often started spontaneously led to interesting initiatives, such as the Leiden Materials Science Centre. Leiden's chemists participate in the Dutch Institute for Catalysis Research, the Holland Research School of Molecular Chemistry, and the Delft-Leiden Graduate Research School of Biotechnological Sciences (BSDL).

In biology, the number of research teams was reduced from twelve to six in the early 1980s: three within zoology, as well as botany, the National Herbarium, and the Institute of Theoretical Biology. In 1989, the National Her-

◄ *Lipsius Building, the central facilities building in the Witte Singel/Doelen complex*

barium, in combination with the university's botanical gardens, acquired the status of research institute. One year later, the Institute of Molecular Botany was founded. The work being done on evolutionary research led to another research line at the Institute of Evolutionary and Ecological Sciences. Finally, the Centre for Biopharmaceutical Sciences is emphatically not a training course for pharmacists, but a research course, which collaborates intensively with the pharmaceutics industry. Collaboration with the Academic Hospital led in 1987 to the founding of the Centre for Human Drug Research. Finally, the research institute known as Leiden/Amsterdam Centre for Drug Research was set up jointly with the Free University, and in 1992, it joined with a number of foreign partners to found a consortium of what has since grown to five pharmaceutical laboratories.

Social Sciences

The effects of specialisation and growth meant that by 1975, the faculty of social sciences (founded in 1963) consisted of 22 departments with academic staff from seven disciplines, active in four subfaculties (sociology, cultural anthropology and sociology of non-Western societies, psychology, child and adult education), as well as in an inter-faculty department of political sciences. What is more, the faculty was housed in a dozen centres and institutes, some of them a considerable distance apart. To make matters more complex still, since the introduction of the University Administration (Reform) Act (WUB), subfaculties had been responsible for decision-making. This was truly a divided realm.

The spectacular growth in student numbers, especially in child education and psychology, combined with the shorter duration of degree courses, called not only for tighter programming but also for a reorganisation. Major procedures such as the Subject Specialization and Concentration Operation (TVC) and the Selective Shrinkage and Growth Operation (SKG) brought dramatic changes, mergers between departments and entire subfaculties (child education and psychology), and most dramatically of all, the loss of sociology

▶ *Central hall, Lipsius Building*

for Leiden, aside from a basic facility, in exchange (with Rotterdam) for political science.

The other major development in this period was the founding in 1978 and subsequent expansion of the Social Sciences Research Service (DSWO), a money-maker with a unique format. Of the faculty's 191 members of staff in 1983, a hundred were paid for by direct government funding, eleven through indirect funding mechanisms, and an astonishing eighty through contract research – the so-called 'third flow of funds'. Spectacular though these figures were, much of this contract work was either not particularly ground-breaking or specifically Dutch in its focus. It was eventually decided that contract research funding would be accepted only if the work concerned was of demonstrable value to the research that received direct government funding. At the end of the 1980s, the DSWO was gradually dismantled, and from its resources was created a new faculty research institute (LISWO), to which four of the eight original teams were transferred.

In 1989, the faculty was relocated in the former outpatient clinic for internal medicine. The building was named after the seventeenth-century Leiden cloth merchant Pieter de la Court – after a contest had been held to find a name. The choice attracted censure from progressive quarters, probably because De la Court, a friend of the great statesman De Witt's and a fascinating writer on theoretical political economics, was described in encyclopaedias as a 'spokesman of the new class of capitalist burghers'. This comical fray perhaps symbolised the inability of the building to moderate the relative autonomy of the various departments, each of which took possession of a separate floor.

This phenomenon – which, as we have seen, was common to all disciplines – was reinforced in FSW by the sharp split between humanities and science among the spectrum of courses it offered. Subjects clearly belonging to the humanities, such as religious anthropology and philosophical sociology, had little in common with scientific disciplines such as theory of functions (a branch of experimental psychology), or research on elections or citations. But it was these latter subjects that would gradually determine the faculty's profile. With the loss of sociology and the study of adult education, added to

◄ *Former Botanical Laboratory, now P.J. Veth Building for departments of non-Western languages and cultures* the growing comparativist and quantitative emphasis in the science of public administration and political science and the shift within child education (caused partly by the disappearance of disciplines such as child sociology and intercultural child education) towards the significance of neural aspects of child behaviour, the faculty appears to have come down on the science side of the fence. Most notably in the behavioural sciences, psychology and educational sciences, interest in neuro-scientific issues has led to growing collaboration with LUMC research teams.

Law

Law too was a wide-ranging faculty in the 1970s, offering a wide variety of courses. Besides the course leading to a master's degree in Dutch law, within which students could specialise in civil, constitutional, administrative, criminal or commercial law, Leiden had separate courses in fiscal and notarial law, as well as three politically oriented courses (public administration, political science, and international law). It also included unique research institutes for papyrology, Eastern European law, and the law of non-Western societies (the Van Vollenhoven Institute). Finally, although Leiden did not have an economics faculty, there was an influential economics department within its law faculty.

The faculty also had its problems: old and dilapidated buildings, very unfavourable staff-student ratios, and a relatively stingy allocation of research resources. This faculty also had a strong tendency to form separate little realms. Starting in the 1980s, efforts were made to define a core curriculum and core disciplines. The effect was to emphasise subjects relating to positive law at the expense of meta-legal fields such as the philosophy and sociology of law, legal history and economic law, and even of the political science course that had so recently been launched with the social science faculty.

The ultimate goal was to achieve the right mixture, and the main step in this direction was taken in 2001, with the policy document 'De weg naar de kern' ('The Path to the Centre'). This document contains manifest echoes of the general debate on profiles, with a similar emphasis on academic attitudes, a structure geared towards disciplines, and the cohesiveness between teaching and research. Still, there is a difference of vantage-point. The faculty is well aware that it is an educationally-oriented part of a largely research-driven university. As an academic discipline, it therefore focuses first and foremost on major subjects such as civil and corporate law, and the somewhat smaller but influential subjects of fiscal and notarial law, criminal and administrative law, and European and international law. In other words, it focuses on subjects – like civil and international law in particular – which are among Leiden's traditional strengths.

To improve the integration of teaching and to monitor its quality, the Cleveringa Institute was established in 2001. Unity and cooperation became major evaluation criteria, including firm structural integration with research and practical application. Every master's degree course includes a tutorial heavily oriented towards cultivating research skills and a practical course revolving around the professional skills required for legal practice and criminology.

The faculty's research was moved to the E.M. Meijers Institute in 1997. This institute was born from the idea that important research fields lie precisely along the lines dividing disciplines. Thus, the research was classified not so much by department but according to themes like legal uniformity, equality before the law, and the predictability of the law, for society as a whole as well as for individuals. 'Binding decision-making' became the central concept in the research programme, at the level of legislature and court, central and local authority as well as at the level of civil parties, and between states and international agencies.

Finally, the faculty needed to formulate a response to the trend of increasing internationalisation, even in areas with a traditionally national focus. In 2003, it was decided to establish a Strategic Alliance of Research Faculties of Law, in which ten European law faculties (including Bologna, Leuven, Oxford and Heidelberg) collaborate to arrange exchanges and expert meetings. There is also the Grotius Centre for International Legal Studies within The Hague Campus.

◄ *Display case with waders in the National Museum of Natural History (Rijksmuseum Naturalis)*
▲ *Specimens prepared by Bernard Albinus and a drawing by Jan Wandelaar, in the teaching wing of Leiden University Medical Centre (LUMC)*

Around the same time, the long-standing problems with shortage of space were finally being resolved. In 2004, the law faculty was able to move into the Kamerlingh Onnes building, the former laboratory, now converted into a gleaming new unit location, equipped with fine classrooms, a splendid library and first-class ICT facilities. In 2000, a faculty chronicler had recorded his gloomy reflections under the heading 'Room for improvement'. Seven years later, the improvements were plain to see.

Humanities

The archipelago of Leiden's humanities is of a size and diversity of subject matter that is unparalleled within the university. If Phaedrus was right that *'varietas delectat'* (variety pleases), this not even particularly large faculty must radiate enough charm for all the rest of the university put together. Amid this variety, significant common denominators can be identified. The first is the faculty's division into 'Western' and 'non-Western' sections. Then there is a separate, threefold division on methodological grounds. While the Western languages have retained the subject-oriented differentiation between linguistics and literature, the 'non-Western' sections have tended to adopt a regional focus, combining existing subjects with historical disciplines or social sciences. Third, there are the specific historical disciplines of history and art history, which have a long-established tendency to combine chronological and geographical as well as philological and sociological perspectives. Very recently, a debate arose within the faculty on devising a new structure geared towards the postgraduate phase, with a division into five institutes. According to this model, history, art history, linguistics and literature would each acquire institutes of their own, besides which a fifth 'regional' institute would be created.

The 'Western' sections have largely adhered to courses in specialised subjects. Besides courses in specific languages, the faculty offers courses in history and art history. There are also two notable exceptions: Greek and Latin languages and cultures (GLTC), and the languages and cultures of Latin Amer-

▲ *Vacuum pump and Leiden flasks belonging to Van Musschenbroek, in Museum Boerhaave.*

● *Specimens prepared by Albinus (Anatomy Museum) and Ahmes sarcophagus (National Museum of Antiquities)*

▼ *The Egyptian Taffeh Temple in the National Museum of Antiquities. Peasant woman, painted on silk in the early nineteenth century by Utagawa Toyokuni (1769-1825) in the Siebold House*

ica (TCLA). The core subjects of the teaching programme in GLTC are ancient
history, philosophy and classical archaeology, while in TCLA, which was created after reorganisations had deprived Leiden of its Spanish department,
there is a chair in history as well as chairs in linguistics and literature. In this
department too, research has been assigned to national research institutes,
such as the Holland Institute for Linguistics, OIKOS for classical studies, and a
number of multidisciplinary institutes such as the Leiden Institute for the
modern period.

The great difference in the way the 'Oriental' sections operate can probably be ascribed to a difference in background. Unlike the Western subjects'
purely philological parent discipline, which was by its very nature oriented
towards the past, the emphasis on practical matters that has long figured
prominently in Oriental studies has yielded a tendency to explore links with
the contemporary era and contextual factors. In this area too, Leiden has
sought to highlight continuity rather than modernity, and the area studies
carried out there all contain a sizeable philological and/or historical component. In the 1980s, a proposal was put forward to combine all area studies in a
single faculty, but this proved not to be feasible. More successful was the proposal to found a Centre of Non-Western Studies, building on the success of
the course in the languages and cultures of Latin America. This new Centre
(CNWS) achieved recognition as a research school in 1994 under the name of
School of Asian, African, and Amerindian Studies. Not long afterwards, Leiden also acquired an International Institute of Asian Studies and an International Institute for the Study of Islam.

The history department has held fast to the traditional division into antiquity, Middle Ages, Dutch, general and socioeconomic history. Several history
professorships exist outside the history department, in Asian studies. This
gives the faculty a unique profile, and necessarily means close cooperation
with 'Non-Western studies'. Art history has always been a smaller department. Its initial emphasis on iconology, with its renowned, independently developed documentation system Iconclass, was gradually divided up, with an
emphasis on the Renaissance on the one hand and applied arts on the other.
Relatively recent additions are the chair in architectural history and the posi-

tion of senior lecturer in Early Christian art, both of which were created in 1971. The latter was abolished in 1996 in favour of a chair in modern art.

The Smaller Faculties Theology, Philosophy, Archaeology and the Arts

Ever since the 1876 Higher Education Act, the theology faculty had operated according to a dual structure, some of the subjects being taught by university staff, while others were the responsibility of the Dutch Reformed Church and the Remonstrant Brotherhood. The 'state-taught' subjects were Old and New Testament, ecclesiastical history, systematic subjects, social sciences and religious history. The Church-taught subjects included dogmatic theology, Christian ethics, and subjects related to pastoral practice. In 1992, a course on Islamic studies was founded, followed in 1999 by a 'world religions' programme. The faculty's research focused primarily on the textual history of the Old Testament, the tradition of ideas between Judaism and early Christianity, patristic and irenic theology, and the relationship between Protestantism and the Enlightenment. The Leiden faculty took part in the Dutch research school for theology and religious studies, which achieved formal recognition in 1994, and founded its own Leiden Institute for the Study of Religion, which was also recognised in 1994.

Philosophy in Leiden, artificially inflated to Central Interfaculty under the terms of the 1960 Act, only to be deflated again to Faculty of Philosophy under the legislation of 1992, has a strong traditional bias towards philosophical semantics. Its teaching takes in a large proportion of systematic philosophy, but its primary research areas are ancient philosophy, the history of logic and semantics, and philosophical interpretation in the tradition of Hegel, Nietzsche and Heidegger. In addition, an important research programme was set up at the interface of epistemology, philosophy of science, cognitive psychology and the history of contemporary philosophy.

With the opening of the Archaeology Centre at Reuvensplaats, some of Leiden's varied archaeological disciplines were brought together under one roof. Six degree courses were eventually defined: prehistory, classical archaeology, Near East, Indian America, Southeast Asia and archaeological sciences. Research was conducted across a very wide spectrum. Within the Netherlands, it focused mainly on traces of inhabitation dating from the Iron Age and the Roman era, to the *Bandkeramik* culture and the early Neanderthalers. But large-scale excavations are also conducted in the Jordan valley, the Caribbean region, Guadeloupe and Niger. Classical archaeology emphasised the urbanisation of the pre-Roman era and studied artistic production in its architectural and social context. In 1992 the research school ARCHON was founded as a national joint venture, achieving recognition by the Royal Academy of Arts and Sciences in 1996.

Finally, besides focusing on students with two or more talents, the arts faculty also enriches the curriculum by providing reciprocal optional subjects. The strength of this cooperation between university and academy appears to lie in the development of new major-minor courses of study. Incorporated into the general studies course, this broad, general component of the curriculum fulfils its original purpose more than in the past. For the rest, the faculty also devised a number of research programmes of its own, on the transformation of art and culture and on media technology.

The smaller faculties were finally disbanded in 2008. It was decided to redistribute the faculties and to create clusters of graduate schools in keeping with Leiden's chosen image of 'research university'. The nine existing schools were reduced to five: arts and humanities, law school, science, social and behavioural sciences, and Leiden University Medical Centre. At the same time, the number of faculties was reduced to five, and it seems likely that archaeology will join Science in the not too distant future, the others being subsumed into the Graduate School of Arts and Humanities.

A Handful of Institutes

Although the organigram of a university may look like a reasonable structural entity, it is really, of course, a historically evolved maze. If you surf to the

Dutch version of Leiden University's website and click on 'Organisation', for instance, you find not only the executive board, deans, supervisory board and university council, but also the administrative office and 'expertise centres'. These are innovations dating from 1999, but they have a respectable history; the university's secretariat can be traced all the way back to the sixteenth-century town clerk Jan van Hout. In fact, the abolition of this secretariat was something of a small managerial revolution.

The office set up in 1973, after the introduction of the University Administration (Reform) Act (WUB), was intended as a support unit for the executive board and university council. The secretary was to be responsible for provid-

▲   *Lipsius Building overlooking the Singel canal*

ing services and coordination. But since the various bodies operated with considerable autonomy, coordination continued to pose a difficulty, and the secretary's function did not develop as had been hoped. The period of the first secretary, D.P. den Os (1983-1993) was plagued by cuts. It stood out for a trend towards decentralisation in favour of the faculties combined with an accumulation of more responsibilities, an inauspicious mix that produced many plans for modifications without yielding any solutions. With the appointment of the new secretary, W.L.C.H.M. van den Berg, there was finally an adminis-

▲ *Entrance to the University Library*
▶ *University Library on the canal side*

trative office *for* the university, as well as a separate facilities service (catering, mailroom, printing service, computer-related tasks, building maintenance). Management and policy were finally separated for good. Policy was in the hands of an administrative office working on behalf of the executive board, while management and facilities were entrusted to expertise centres for the entire university.

An International Office was set up, in addition to seven expertise centres: ICS (Information, communication and students), an ICT group, an institute for knowledge transfer (Leiden University Research and Innovation Services), services for facilities and property management, and the university library. Although the library may sound a little 'old' in this context, with its new premises and online catalogue it is a modern organisation with two aims: making available a number of unique and internationally renowned collections (Oriental manuscripts, Western printed material) and making books, journals and other information sources accessible to staff and students. The role of these other information sources is rapidly outstripping that of paper. This, combined with a lack of space, has reduced the acquisitions of monographs and journals from a kilometre a year of shelf space in the 1980s to about 250 metres a year now. This trend is offset by a rapid expansion in the number of digital library services.

Besides faculties, the university also has a number of inter-faculty institutes, such as the Centre for Business Sciences, the School of Asian, African and Amerindian Studies, Leiden Institute for Brain and Cognition, and the Netherlands Institute for the Study of Crime and Law Enforcement. Also operating under its auspices are the Interfaculty Centre for Teacher Training, Education Development and Continuing Education and the Institute of Environmental Sciences. In addition, the university has a large number of inter-university institutes, from the African Studies Centre to the Thomas Stieltjes Institute for Mathematics, most of which are research institutes, but which also include bodies such as the Netherlands Institute in Rome and the Netherlands-Flemish Institute in Cairo.

Finally, the website lists numerous other facilities, from the Academic Historical Museum, the Faculty Club and the Studium Generale organisation to Plexus student centre, 'Kattekop' children's daycare facility, and the university sports centre. Two of them have a long, interesting history and have done much to mould the university's image. The first is Leiden Academic Arts Centre, originally founded for the 'aesthetic development of the university population', which in 1971 moved into an abandoned blanket factory that gave it the perfect shabby ambience for the progressive arts climate of the 1970s. The facilities building in the Witte-Singel Doelen complex endowed the theatre with a completely different atmosphere, most notably more professional, although it operates largely with volunteers. The Arts Centre provides a wide variety of courses, today ranging from Gregorian chants and African dance to the creative use of language.

The second prominent facility, the university's newspaper *Mare*, was founded in 1977 as the successor to *Acta et agenda*. Besides being the forum in which renowned writers such as Maarten Biesheuvel, Boudewijn Buch and Maarten 't Hart aired their unsettling reflections, the paper also became an experimental garden for talented journalists, launching many on careers that continued in the national quality press. It also developed a rather peevish relationship with student life and administrative bodies, frequently describing the former in terms of mere excess and the latter as an outdated machinery redolent of bygone regent days. In sounding out the limits of each other's sense of humour, the newspaper and university are still far from arriving at a harmonious entente.

University and the Business World

Since 1985, providing services to the community and the business world has ranked among the university's core tasks. Many services to society have long been embedded in academia. The LUMC with its patient care and its research geared towards improving health care, the humanities faculty with its annual Huizinga Lecture, the law faculty with its Cleveringa professorship, the social science faculty with its centres set up to research social tensions within society and ways of improving crisis management, they all make their own broad contributions to the society at large. In addition, numerous experts and columnists attached to the university make their presence felt in social debate.

At least as important as these contributions are the university's changing relations with the business community. For many years these relations were poor, with aloofness and mistrust predominating over appreciation and cooperation. The turning-point came with the publication of the 1979 Innovation Memorandum, which encouraged the university to develop ties with the commercial sector, especially with small and medium-sized businesses, and provided for new 'transfer points' set up specifically for this purpose.

These ties were also important to the university, yielding lucrative work that in time yielded a sizeable proportion of its revenue. The university is funded by three 'flows of funds'. The first consists of money allocated directly by the central government, while the second is money allocated indirectly, most notably through the Netherlands Organisation for Scientific Research or bodies derived from it. The 'third flow of funds' consists of money from a variety of sources: the business world, government bodies (national, provincial and municipal), international organisations such as Fullbright, NATO, EU, and the Rockefeller Foundation, and charities such as the Kidney Foundation, the Heart Foundation, and the Wilhelmina Fund. The decision to seek support from the commercial sector did not arise solely from a change in attitudes among staff and students and the growing demand for close relations in the commercial sector itself. It was also something of a necessity, given financial and personnel cuts imposed in the late 1970s, especially in the Medical Faculty and the Faculty of Mathematics and Physics.

This support takes a variety of forms: grants for fundamental research, contract research, preliminary recommendations, advisory positions and suchlike. It also includes money received for the rent of space and facilities, and the proceeds arising from sales of courses, licences and patents. A special Transfer Point was set up in 1981, in collaboration with Delft College (now University) of Technology. It helped potential clients to find the appropriate researcher or research team, supported researchers in their efforts to commercialise their inventions or to find the right partners in industry, and ad-

▶ *Students' course selection festival in St Peter's Church*

vised the executive board about activities relating to the third flow of funds. In collaboration with the Municipality of Leiden and the Chamber of Commerce, the Transfer Point helped to found the Academic Business Centre, which eventually led to the building of the new Science Park in Leeuwenhoek. Specific projects included the university's collaborative framework with Delft on biotechnology and the activities of the Leiden Centre for Biopharmaceutical Sciences.

To streamline these activities more effectively, a task group on the exploitation of knowledge potential was set up in 1995, acquiring institutional status the following year as 'Leiden University Institutional Development' or LUID. The Leiden University Research and Innovation Services was established as an implementing body, to provide the necessary commercial and legal expertise and contacts. A parallel structure is the LUMC's specific 'valorisation' function, the activities of which are attuned to one another. Together, the university and LUMC managed to establish major projects outside the first flow of funds, such as the Centre for Medical Systems Biology and Cyttron for bio-imaging techniques. In addition, LUID established a real holding in 1996 under the name of Libertatis Ergo. This body possesses independent legal personality and has set up several successful companies, including Archol BV for archaeology research, most notably in the route planned for the new Betuweroute freight railway line, a Crisis research Team, Screentec and Heartcore.

The Science Park focused primarily on biomedical and life sciences. Forty companies are based there, half of the specialised life science companies in the Netherlands. Those most closely involved consolidated their ties in 2003 under the slogan of 'Leiden: Life Meets Science'. The Hague Campus, a similar initiative, concentrates mainly on courses in public administration and tailor-made courses developed for the public sector. As a result of these activities, faculties obtained a significant proportion of their budget from the second and third flows of funds in the period 2001-2003: for mathematics and the natural sciences this proportion was 29%, for social sciences it was 19%, for law 14%, for the humanities 13%, and for both archaeology and theology 10%.

Internationalisation

Since the 1970s, the university has also stepped up its efforts to internationalise its research and education. Besides the existing network of individual research contacts, and the incorporation of internships and fieldwork, the university also has an International Centre, founded in 1967. It did not start devising a real policy on internationalisation until 1969, however, with the appointment of a standing committee on foreign ties, set up both to promote

▲   *Palaeontology student at work*

international academic relations and to encourage foreign students to study in Leiden – and vice versa.

Initially, the ideas underlying this initiative were indisputably idealistic: the desire to help solve problems related to issues such as the environment, poverty and war. But a more pragmatic aim also came into play: to break with the tradition of one-way academic traffic by encouraging academics to get involved with foreign institutes. One example is the working group (later Institute) for the history of European expansion (IGEER), founded in 1975. Similar initiatives included the postdoctoral training courses organised by the Department of the Languages and Cultures of Southeast Asia, which were taught partly in Leiden and partly in Indonesia. The re-establishment of cultural ties with Indonesia in 1968 also inspired a range of collaborative projects involving linguistics, cultural history and sociology.

The existence of collections such as that of the National Museum of Ethnology has long been a major source of inspiration, and the university also developed closer relations with para-university institutes such as the Netherlands Institute for the Near East, the African Studies Centre and the Royal Netherlands Institute of Southeast Asian and Caribbean Studies (LITLV), which acquired permanent premises in Leiden in 1967. New collections were formed, for instance for the Documentation Centre for Modern China (since 1965) and IGEER. Other additions included the Institute for Asian Studies, the Indonesia-Netherlands Cooperation Programme for Islamic Studies, and the Centre for International Legal Cooperation.

As a result, major foreign cultural institutes such as those in Jakarta, Cairo and Tokyo, which had been leading a sober or almost threatened existence, acquired a new lease of life. In Cairo, courses for students of Arabic or archaeology were set up, within a cooperative framework involving a number of Flemish universities. The Japan-Netherlands Institute in Tokyo inaugurated the postdoctoral Japan Prize Winners Programme for twenty gifted students. In addition, official representatives were appointed in certain countries, people whose long years of experience with the country in question made them supremely able to promote the interests of Leiden University in that country.

All this called for a change in orientation. The emphasis shifted away from

◄ *Biochemistry student operating NMR apparatus*

development cooperation towards support for education and research. From Brussels, support largely targeted interdisciplinary research, with mobility programmes such as ERASMUS (European Action Scheme for the Mobility of Students), followed by LEONARDO, ISEP and TEMPUS, acronyms for various grants, and meant that Leiden too benefited from a large influx of foreign students, besides being able to send many of its own students around the world.

Looking forward to ERASMUS, Leiden signed a joint venture agreement with a number of traditional universities in 1985, most of them long-established European institutions, to form the Coimbra Group, over which it presided from 1986 to 1997. The idea was that the 20-odd affiliated universities would admit each other's students without charging tuition fees. In 1993, Leiden joined forces with Oxford to found EUROPEUM, an 'international university without walls', in which ten universities participate today. The cooperation has been largely concentrated in the spheres of education and research, mainly in the social sciences, the humanities and research policy.

As a result, the internationalisation of education at Leiden soared to unprecedented heights in the period 1985-1995. In the academic year 1994-95, a staggering 21% of those studying for a master's degree spent one or more terms at a foreign university. At this time, Leiden University itself maintained about ninety bilateral contacts, besides being linked to about two hundred other potential programmes through various groups and grant programmes.

Student Life

'*Sous les pavés la plage*' was the utopian battle-cry with which the students took to the streets of Paris in May 1968. Beneath the paving-stones of civilisation they hoped to find the soft seashore; from beneath the hardened calluses of capitalism would emerge the beating heart of humanity. Forty years later, the street is just the street again, with its slightly pejorative overtones, and while the beach holds a certain appeal, it cannot compete with a café terrace. And on that terrace, students are served by other students. If there is one telling picture that encapsulates the silent revolution that has taken place in

▲ *Student society administrative officials at the opening of the academic year*

student life since the 1970s, it is that of the terrace, a perpetuum mobile where students in general both earn and spend their money, both work and relax, and are in fact no longer students at all.

Because that is what has happened, since the turbulent 1960s and 1970s and the calm 1980s and 1990s: students have become citizens closely committed to the world around them, albeit this commitment means something very different today than it meant forty years ago. According to Karl Marx, all that philosophers had done was to provide different interpretations of the world. What mattered was not to interpret but to *change* the world. Today's students have moved in the opposite direction. Instead of a burning desire to change society, they now demonstrate a perfect ability to adjust to their surroundings – to the world of capitalism and the laws of market forces.

It is revealing to glance down a list of the activities provided by Leiden University's Adult Education Centre, which opened its doors in 1971. The October 1980 issue of the university paper *Mare* lists a total of thirty-three activities, ranging from working groups (on Chemistry and Society, Environmental Management, Indonesia, Women's History, War and Peace) and action groups (Stop the Neutron Bomb, Boycott Outspan Oranges, Abolish Poverty, Amnesty International) to trade unions and pressure groups. Also operating under its auspices were Leiden's legal advice centre and science shop, the chemistry shop, various faculty clubs (for medics, biologists, and political scientists) and a mix of educational activities, and political and religious clubs. Finally, there were activities designed to bolster women's rights and tutoring services. What is more, of course, there was the superb Leiden Academic Arts Centre.

Not only the diversity of this educational work but its sheer volume – the above list is far from exhaustive – shows that the students passionately wanted not just to know themselves and the surrounding world but also to influence them. Such passion seems to be in short supply among the student population at Leiden University today. This change is generally described as a trend towards greater individualisation and pragmatism. Today's students are far more concerned with opportunities for individual profit or personal pleasure, it is said, than those of twenty years ago. They are more interested in training than education; they want to acquire skills not so much to benefit society but to further their own careers. While the student society once organised debating clubs and pressure groups, today it provides excursions to businesses and job markets.

This trend is linked to a shift in the makeup of the student population and changes in the system of student grants and loans. The population has changed in two respects: socially, from extremely diverse to fairly homogeneous, and in terms of gender, from primarily male to evenly balanced between the sexes. Cuts in student grants compel most students to take jobs to supplement their income. All this means that student life is no longer a distinctive, separate part of society. In the 1970s, 'ordinary' young people had little contact with students. These days, students are scarcely distinguishable from the rest of what is now called youth culture.

Leiden's students also seem to have resolved the old moral dilemmas associated with sex and politics. Condom dispensers have given way to serial monogamy, every society now has its own gay club and female administrators, and students no longer appear to feel the need for a Women's Network such as the one that had existed at the university since 1984. Interest in committee work and the university council has plummeted, and the student turnout in recent university elections has slumped below 30%. This does not mean that politics has lost its appeal to Leiden's students, but merely that their interests tend to have a more national focus.

All this could easily be demonstrated on the basis of a brief history of Leiden's various social clubs. There is no room for this in the present short account; at best, a brief impression can be given of the diversity of student life, for all the trends fostering unity. Besides relatively old societies such as Leiden Student Fraternity and the society for women students (VVSL), Augustinus (Catholic) and SSR (Protestant), in 1952 the society Catena was founded, which emphatically broke with stale ideas on the community spirit and extended a welcoming hand to non-religious fraternity members. Over the years, this small society has always maintained its rather non-conformist profile.

In the 1960s, the two religious student societies both cut loose from their

confessional moorings for good, although what one describes as 'humanism' and the other as 'a sense of home' still evoke historical connotations. They initially seemed to be so open to the wider community as to be forfeiting their student identity altogether, but this process was reversed in the 1980s with a renewed focus on clubs for specific cohorts of students and debating clubs. This 'studenty' atmosphere certainly permeated Quintus, the new, fifth student society, founded in 1969. Quintus started life as something of a parasite, draining the memberships of the other societies with 'the primacy of inexorable conviviality'. But with the passage of time, the other clubs became more convivial and Quintus lost its distinctive ambience.

The atmosphere and flavour of Leiden's student life are still determined today, at least to the eyes of the outside world, by the largest society, Minerva, which was born in 1972 from a merger between the fraternity and vvSL. This largest and oldest of all the student societies effortlessly sustains popular prejudices regarding the students. Whether they go about sporting jackets and ties and trousers with turned-up hems or twin sets and penny-shoes, people will say that a member of Minerva can be spotted from a mile off. In fact such identification has often proved unexpectedly difficult, although even in the heyday of long hair and beards, this dress code was seldom favoured by fraternity members.

Besides its social clubs and societies, Leiden has had numerous subject-based debating clubs and societies since the nineteenth century. These are still characteristic of student life, in that their activities are still modelled on the organisational structure and *modus operandi* of the Senate and the university itself. Department-based societies have directed their efforts towards improving the curriculum (making it easier to study), and organising the reception of first-year students, including the 'El Cid' introductory programme, and student mentorships. These societies now also take pride in their conviviality, as do the debating clubs. Most are in the humanities and the arts, and some are of a venerable age. Their core activities, making speeches and criticising each other's work, seem to hold out ever less appeal to first-year students, however, so that even they seem set to cultivate conviviality as a last resort.

◄ *Doorbells, student house*

Our Quirks

Skills and expertise need traditions, in the exact sciences just as much as in the humanities. This is the central proposition put forward by Edward Shils in his book *Tradition*. The university's own self-image adds another dimension: customs are more varied and observed with more intensity here than elsewhere. Finally, the permanent process of change to which universities have been exposed for the last hundred years has led automatically to the 'invention' of new traditions. This occurs more frequently, explain Hobsbawm and Ranger, in their book *The Invention of Tradition*, 'when a rapid transformation of society weakens or destroys the social patterns for which "old" traditions had been designed.' Such traditions symbolise social cohesion, confirm membership of natural or artificial groups, and lend legitimacy to an institution's status.

Leiden's student community provides a good illustration of this process. From a population that was once completely disparate in terms of age, background and origin, that had little to do with the city and not very much to do with the rest of the university, a close-knit student fraternity evolved in the course of the nineteenth century, which sought recognition from the body of professors, and also from the local townspeople. The students modelled their societies on existing university constructions: first-year initiation rituals were based on doctorate ceremonies, and procedure in student debating clubs was based on that in the body of professors. Students took on voluntary military service, they organised masquerades, city festivals and concerts for the poor; they developed countless customs that promoted internal cohesiveness and consolidated the ties between town and gown.

In the historical development of the university's image, the evolution of its internal customs is therefore very revealing. A key feature of a student society was its reading table. In its eagerness to duplicate learned societies in the outside world, Leiden's student fraternity created a reading table of impressive abundance. Around 1900, no fewer than 93 newspapers and periodicals could be consulted at Minerva's reading table, 33 of which were in a foreign

▶ *Student house on Rapenburg canal*

language. These 93 included 25 daily newspapers, while of the remaining publications, 25 were recreational, 25 targeted a broad intellectual readership and 18 were scholarly or scientific. It was this table that was to become the arena of social emancipation at the end of the century. The debates on the procurement of social-democrat periodicals shattered the university's ivory towers, and the magazines were ordered, but they were often found torn to pieces on the floor under the reading table.

Even today, many customs revolve around the reading table, although few have anything to do with reading. One popular form of entertainment is 'lifting the reading table'. The table is also used for beer-drinking relay races called 'bulb drinking', which consists of downing a large lamp-globe filled with beer as quickly as possible. The furthest removed from the table's original purpose is 'page sliding', which involves resting the reading table at an angle against the banister. A brake path of smaller tables is added, and the idea is to slide down this structure on a tray. Another pastime, in which the table is the object of a kind of tug-of-war between students of different years, seems equally hard to reconcile with reading.

From these downright antithetical applications, another aspect of the students' *mores* can be inferred, namely a mode of self-irony. For instance, Leiden University's long-standing ties with the Royal House are entwined with other reading-table customs. The table is also known as *agora*, and anyone who wants to hold forth about something can use the table as his soap-box. It will cost him a bottle of champagne to do so, unless he manages to open the bottle in such a way that the cork hits the pane of glass protecting the Alexander goblet. In other words, if he comes close to damaging a gift from the Royal House, the student can proclaim his views free of charge.

The familiarity with which 'Her Majesty's First', as the Leiden student fraternity calls itself, treats the Royal House is also clear from the existence of so-called *lippjes*. After Prince Bernhard (whose last name was Von *Lippe* Biesterfeld) flouted the ban on resting one's feet on the low hearth table, small extensible strips of wood were attached to the table for this very purpose. These became known as *lippjes*. Fourth-year and more senior students are even permitted to put plates of food on these *lippjes*.

The university itself maintains a custom that is directly related to the Royal House: it sends the monarch a telegram announcing the celebrations of its foundation day, which are also held in honour of the university's founder, William of Orange. Formerly, the university senate would adopt the text of the telegram on the morning of the *Dies*, and the reply received in the afternoon could be read out during the senate dinner. But since neither senate nor senate dinner exists today, it is now the executive board that sends the telegram and the rector who reads out the answer at the end of the foundation day ceremony. Sometimes the reply has not yet been received by then, in which case someone will solemnly ask what has happened to it.

There are also negative customs, and these too help to define the university's identity. For instance, until a few decades ago, Leiden's rector did not have a chain of office. This omission was intended to reflect the unity and equality that characterised the professors as members of the senate. It had an amusing side-effect, however, since in a group of rectors from universities in the rest of the country, it was Leiden's rector who stood out, as the only one not wearing a chain. In other countries, however, this simplicity proved less effective, and the rector was often taken for an ordinary professor who had lost his way. Eventually these misunderstandings came to be regarded as tiresome, and a chain of office was introduced in the early 1970s.

Leiden held firm to its formal dress, however, the simplest of all gowns. The official rules on dress date from 1877. In that year it was laid down by royal decree that for public doctoral ceremonies and other formal occasions, professors must wear black silk gowns and a black velvet cap, over 'black garments and white tie and bands'. In Leiden, it was decided at some unknown point in time to discreetly 'overlook' the part about the bands. In fact, the former rector Cohen, who wrote a brief chronicle of Leiden's customs, recalls an occasion on which a colleague from another university who entered the senate chamber in his formal robes prior to a doctoral ceremony was told in no uncertain terms by those around him 'Take those bands off!'.

The ceremony surrounding the conferral of a doctorate also has its special customs. For instance, when the beadle enters the hall and pronounces the words '*hora est*', this ends the proceedings immediately, without the current speaker being permitted to finish his or her sentence. Another custom forbids a PhD candidate thanking the supervising professor in the foreword to his thesis. At the end of a doctoral ceremony or inaugural address held in the main auditorium, 'those seated beneath the organ' – that is, closest to the door – are instructed to remain in their seats until everyone else has left, something that always causes a certain amount of merriment. A new professor making his inaugural address is welcomed in the senate chamber beforehand by the rector, who sums up his fine qualities and then traditionally asks him if he knows where the text of his address is. An affirmative answer is all that is required.

Leiden's ceremonies for the conferral of a master's degree also have their own unwritten rules. When the beadle comes to fetch a student from the small room where he awaits his results in trepidation, the words 'Mr So-and-so *with* those accompanying him' means that the candidate has passed. The very existence of this little room, on the walls of which custom dictates that the successful student may place his signature, is one of the university's most deeply cherished customs. The precise choice of words at a doctoral ceremony is equally significant. If the chairman of the doctoral committee observes that the candidate has provided a 'superb defence of this thesis', the audience know that the distinction *cum laude* (to insiders a *cummetje*) is to be awarded.

The preservation of many such customs came under considerable pressure in the 1960s and 1970s. The large increase in student numbers often made them hard to keep up, and many condemned them as reflecting bourgeois attitudes and repressiveness. One description of the academic gown slated it as part of 'an outmoded, semi-aristocratic, deadly earnest bourgeois ritual'. Opponents traded in black ties and black shoes for strings of beads and sneakers to press home the point. Less radical voices too criticised the surfeit of ritual, one describing Leiden as a 'pre-literary society, where nothing is written down and the elders have the last word'.

Since the late 1980s, the university's traditional customs have enjoyed a conspicuous revival. First of all, the rituals surrounding the conferral of a master's degree were revived. Instead of the rather meagre formalities that had been observed for many years, students were once again expected to turn

▲ *Albert Einstein (1879-1955). Professor of physics by special appointment (1920-1946)*

up to the ceremony dressed to the nines and accompanied by their families. Speeches and champagne, graduation songs and a video record of the graduate's university years, modelled on nineteenth-century precedent, have enjoyed a colourful comeback. Each department opens the academic year with its own ceremony, complete with a procession of professors and a special address. At one point, the dean of the law faculty did his best to get into the *Guinness Book of Records* for having awarded a total of 4,000 degree certificates and having made a speech to accompany every one of them.

This revival of ritual is neither exclusive to Leiden nor exclusive to universities. Still, Leiden University certainly reaps the traditional benefits of this trend in the form of a framework for disagreement, a lack of susceptibility to fashion. 'Nowhere are opinions so deeply divided as there,' recalls one psychologist who left Leiden for Maastricht. 'And yet everyone is accepted, and relations are very relaxed.' Tolerance and liberalism – these are the defining characteristics chosen by many professors coming to Leiden from elsewhere. The Leiden Slavist Karel van het Reve maintained in his farewell speech that it was precisely the university's customs that made it possible that even someone from the ungodly depths of Amsterdam or the proletarian suburb of *Betondorp*, from a communist family, a school with a leftist reputation or an even more leftist university was still welcome at the 'Borobudur of the bourgeoisie'.

It all implied a certain imperviousness to fashion. Van het Reve said that it was as if the customs muffled the way news permeated to Leiden. He recalled one occasion on which the senate's foundation day telegram had been addressed to 'Princess Juliana'; fortunately, someone discovered just in time that she was actually the Queen – and had been for ten years! And Leiden's students once invited the historian Jan Romein to give a lecture, several years after his death, prompting his widow to write back, 'Although I do not make a habit of opening other people's letters …'. The widow of the Leiden physicist Paul Ehrenfest, Tatyana Afanasyeva, once remarked: 'Nowhere does the transition from life to death go unnoticed to the same degree as in Leiden.' It should be added, though, that the words were addressed to Albert Einstein, who felt perfectly at ease in the Leiden of Hendrik Lorentz.

▶ *University flag, administration building*

HENDRIK ANTOON LORENTZ ARNHEMENSIS

NATUS 18 JULII 1853. PROF. PHYS. THEOR. IN
AGAD. LUGD. BAT. 1878. OBIIT HARLEMII 4 FEBR. 1928.

HEIKE KAMERLINGH ONNES. GRONINGENSIS.

NATUS 21 SEPT. 1853. PHYS. EXPER.
PROF. ORD. AC. L.B. 11 NOV. 1882.
OBIIT LEIDAE 21 FEBR. 1926.

JOHAN HUIZINGA GRONINGANUS

ATUS 7 DEC. 1872. PROF. IN ACAD. GRON. 1905~1915. PROF.
HISTORIAE GENERALIS ET GEOGRAPHIAE POLITICAE IN
CAD. LUGDUNO~BATAVA 1915~1942. OBIIT 1 FEBR. 1945

Graphs and Tables

Statistics relating to student numbers and (for recent times) numbers of academic and other staff appear in several parts of this book. Those for student numbers derive from various sources: the figures for the period 1575 to 1875 are based on the Album Studiosorum, in which all students were registered from the university's foundation onwards, and which exists in two printed versions (1575-1875 and 1875-1925). The statistics for the subsequent period are based on the university's yearbooks, while those for the period from 1975 onwards were supplied by the Information Management Department of the Administrative Office.

Although the statistics for the entire period are reasonably comprehensive, comparisons are impeded by constant changes in the names of courses and faculties, the definition of the term 'student', and enrolment policy. The figures have been aligned as well as possible by means of extrapolation and by comparing the different sources. The statistics for members of staff, which were also supplied by the Information Management Department, are based on annual reports.

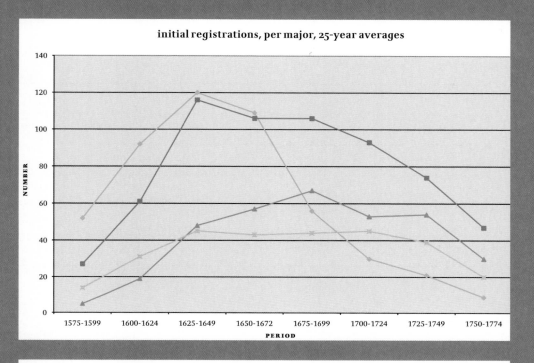

initial registrations, per major, 25-year averages

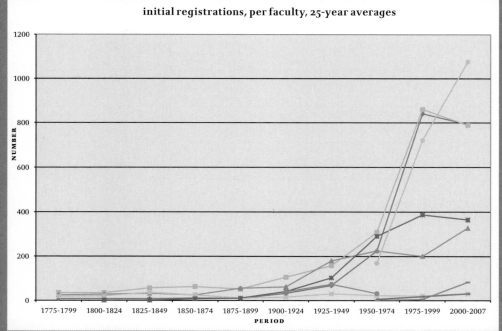

initial registrations, per faculty, 25-year averages

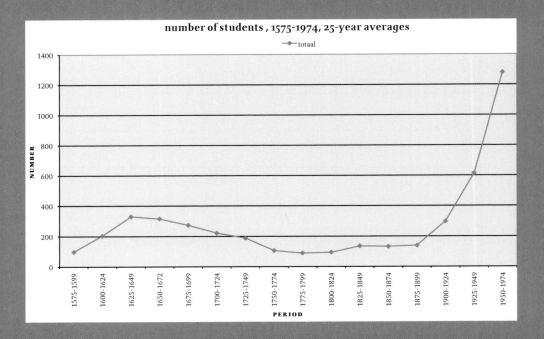

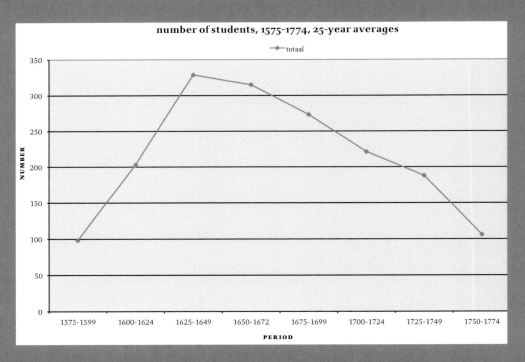

	HUMANITIES	LAW	MEDICINE	THEOLOGY	MATHEMATICS & PHYSICS	LAW & HUMANITIES	SOCIAL SCIENCES	PHILOSOPHY	ARCHAEOLOGY	ART	TOTAL
1575-1599	52	27	5	14							98
1600-1624	92	61	19	31							203
1625-1649	120	116	48	45							329
1650-1672	109	106	57	43							315
1675-1699	56	106	67	44							273
1700-1724	30	93	53	45							221
1725-1749	21	74	54	39							188
1750-1774	9	47	30	20							106
1775-1799	9	36	26	18							89
1800-1824	9	35	28	21	1						94
1825-1849	8	57	32	36	2						135
1850-1874	11	63	25	25	8						132
1875-1899	10	52	55	11	11						139
1900-1924	33	106	62	15	41	40					297
1925-1949	68	158	180	30	103	74					613
1950-1974	225	309	226	22	291	32	168	6	1		1280
1975-1999	841	861	201	21	387		721	18	5		3055
2000-2007	793	789	328	31	365		1076	31	83	4	3500

	THEOLOGY	LAW	MEDICINE	MATHEMATICS & PHYSICS	LIBERAL ARTS	LAW & HUMANITIES	SOCIAL SCIENCES	MATHEMATICS & LIBERAL ARTS	PHILOSOPHY	ARCHAEOLOGY	ART	TOTAL
1950	30	219	258	189	105	94		19				914
1951	34	211	216	154	169	43		20				847
1952	18	194	200	121	105	29		26				693
1953	19	172	137	129	106	27		23				613
1954	19	159	141	126	116	27		15				603
1955	18	157	139	186	141	31		34				706
1956	13	144	147	178	148	41		34				705
1957	15	161	147	197	160	49		53				782
1958	14	166	177	201	179	63		46				846
1959	13	160	181	234	214	64		46				912
1960	13	171	210	248	241	59		51				993
1961	11	201	184	283	242	55		55				1031
1962	19	207	213	293	200	65		66				1063
1963	13	192	238	287	218	82		66				1096
1964	25	255	309	299	272	80		71				1311
1965	26	303	295	367	246		192		9	1		1439
1966	30	414	290	395	255		290		10			1684
1967	28	430	276	399	259		292		5	3		1692
1968	35	394	257	410	252		322		11	3		1684
1969	26	544	327	386	283		337		17	1		1921
1970	20	531	230	434	250		371		14	2		1852
1971	25	609	320	418	370		445		22	2		2211
1972	27	617	320	459	370		429		28	3		2253
1973	31	556	269	438	252		479		23	2		2050
1974	34	555	181	434	471		413		22	0		2110
1975	29	583	179	466	588		448		25	0		2318
1976	33	593	179	512	666		542		21	0		2546
1977	29	755	200	513	727		568		33	0		2825
1978	22	870	185	507	743		566		30	1		2924

	THEOLOGY	LAW	MEDICINE	MATHEMATICS & PHYSICS	LIBERAL ARTS	LAW & HUMANITIES	SOCIAL SCIENCES	MATHEMATICS & LIBERAL ARTS	PHILOSOPHY	ARCHAEOLOGY	ART	TOTAL
1979	22	752	184	467	801		545		11	0		2782
1980	29	763	195	462	797		567		18	0		2831
1981	37	766	180	452	843		546		17	1		2842
1982	17	825	187	407	812		556		18	0		2822
1983	18	980	235	460	859		624		26	5		3207
1984	15	893	188	364	874		512		8	0		2854
1985	26	980	214	373	1016		830		24	0		3463
1986	11	916	207	354	922		649		9	1		3069
1987	19	1028	190	436	1046		843		12	1		3575
1988	11	1054	214	427	1082		839		18	0		3645
1989	19	1086	217	418	1172		1038		22	1		3973
1990	15	1112	202	406	1135		1042		20	0		3932
1991	14	1005	197	312	1063		978		14	0		3583
1992	23	933	206	293	884		860		21			3220
1993	20	858	199	324	843		839		20			3103
1994	13	912	216	288	813		810		14	2		3068
1995	20	923	203	294	730		731		12			2913
1996	28	854	207	288	756		762		9			2904
1997	25	781	216	314	680		730		15	24		2785
1998	12	681	215	281	598		779		17	43		2626
1999	13	631	211	267	577		826		20	51		2596
2000	21	657	252	294	602		903		28	47		2804
2001	22	763	288	313	691		1044		36	78		3235
2002	35	787	317	349	720		1151		34	67		3460
2003	24	894	355	419	803		1321		27	94		3937
2004	32	854	359	349	745		1130		23	95		3587
2005	28	762	360	346	801		1032		37	110	6	3482
2006	42	742	351	418	997		946		27	93	10	3626
2007	41	849	344	431	987		1077		38	77	12	3856

Photo Credits

The illustrations in this book were selected to tell their own story rather than to support – let alone replace – parts of the text. This explains why they are scattered throughout the text, while not entirely at random, certainly not always 'on the spot'.

Academic Historical Museum 24-25, 26, 39, 40, 42, 45, 49, 56, 57, 75, 79, 82-83, 86, 90, 91, 94, 97, 117, 123, 126, 129, 130, 131, 134, 136, 137, 140, 141, 143, 146, 158, 161, 164-165, 167, 168, 169, 172, 173, 174, 177, 178, 182, 186, 188-189, 190-191, 193, 194

Academiegebouw (main university building) 17, 50, 72, 110, 111, 112, 113, 118, 120, 121, 181, 196, 197, 198, 199, 283, 286, 287, 288, 289

Anatomy Museum (LUMC) 102, 103

Jos van den Broek 2, 6, 8, 11, 12, 202, 205, 206, 209, 210, 213, 216, 217, 219, 220, 223, 224, 228, 229, 231, 232, 235, 236-237, 238, 241, 242, 245, 246, 249, 250, 254, 255, 256, 261, 262, 263, 267, 269, 270, 273, 276, 279, 285

Leiden municipal archives 29, 104

Leiden University Library 16, 18, 19, 30, 34, 35, 53, 54, 62, 64, 65, 66, 69, 76, 107

Museum Boerhaave 99

National Museum of Antiquities 60, 149

National Museum of Natural History (Rijksmuseum Naturalis) 150

National Museum of Ethnography 153, 154, 157

National Library of the Netherlands, The Hague 32

Rijksmuseum, Amsterdam 108

Stedelijk Museum de Lakenhal 46

Bibliography

This book is largely based on the three volumes of my history of Leiden University (and on the content of the fourth, which is still in manuscript form). For a detailed bibliography, readers are invited to consult these three earlier volumes of my *Groepsportret met Dame*, viz. *Het bolwerk van de vrijheid. De Leidse universiteit, 1575-1672* (Amsterdam 2000), *De vesting van de macht. De Leidse universiteit, 1673-1775* (Amsterdam 2002) and *De werken van de wetenschap. De Leidse universiteit, 1776-1876* (Amsterdam 2005).

Printed Sources and Bibliographies

Album Studiosorum Academiae Lugduno-Batavae (2 vols., 1575-1875 (The Hague 1875) and 1875-1925 (Leiden 1925)

Album Scholasticum Academiae Lugduno-Batavae (3 vols., 1575-1940 (Leiden 1941), 1940-1974 (Leiden 1975) and 1975-1989 (Leiden 1991)

'Bibliographie selective de l'université de Leiden', R.E.O. Ekkart in *Bibliographie internationale de l'histoire des universités II* (1976) 83-128

Bibliografie van hoogleraren in de rechten aan de Leidse universiteit tot 1811, M. Ahsmann and R. Feenstra (Amsterdam 1984)

Bronnen tot de geschiedenis der Leidsche Universiteit, P.C. Molhuysen (7 vols., The Hague 1913-1924)

Icones Leidenses. De portretverzameling van de Rijksunivrsiteit te Leiden, R.E.O. Ekkart (Leiden 1973)

Leiden Medical Professors 1575-1940 (Leiden 2007)

Academic Context

M. Albrecht, *Eklektik* (Stuttgart 1994)

H.J. Berman, *Law and Revolution. The Formation of the Western Legal Tradition* (Cambridge, MA 1983)

H. Bots and F. Waquet (eds.), *Commercium Litterarium 1600-1750* (Amsterdam 1994)

W. Clark et al. (eds.), *The Sciences in Enlightened Europe* (Chicago 1999)

H. Coing (ed.), *Handbuch der Quellen und Litteratur der neueren Europäischen Privatrechtsgeschichte* (2 vols., Munich 1973, 1977)

P. Dear, *Revolutionizing the Sciences. European Knowledge and its Ambitions, 1500-1700* (Basingstoke 2001)

J.V. Field and F.A.J.L. James (eds.), *Renaissance and Revolution.*

Humanists, Scholars, Craftsmen, and Natural Philosophers in Early Modern Europe (Cambridge 1993)

L.I. Conrad et al. (eds.), *The Western Medical Tradition* (Cambridge 1995)

A. Grafton, *New Worlds, Ancient Texts. The Power of Tradition and the Shock of Discovery* (Cambridge, Mass. 1992)

N. Jardine et al. (eds.), *Cultures of Natural History* (Cambridge 1996)

M. Herberger, *Dogmatik. Zur Geschichte vom Begriff und Methode in Medizin und Jurisprudenz* (Frankfurt am Main 1981)

A. Moss, *Printed Commonplace-Books and the Structuring of Renaissance Thought* (Oxford 1996)

J.V. Pickstone, *Ways of Knowing. A New History of Science, Technology and Medicine* (Manchester 2000)

J. Platt, *Reformed Thought and Scholasticism* (Leiden 1982)

R.H. Popkin, *The History of Scepticism from Erasmus to Descartes* (Assen 1964)

Henning Graf Reventlow, *Epochen der Bibelauslegung* (4 vols., Munich 1990-2001)

Walter Rüegg (general editor), *A History of the University in Europe.* (3 vols., Cambridge 1992, 1996 and 2004).

C.B. Schmitt, *Aristotle and the Renaissance* (Cambridge, MA. 1983)

P. Stein, *The Character and Influence of the Roman Civil Law* (London 1988)

A. Waquet, *Le latin ou l'empire d'un signe 16e-20e siècle* (Paris 1998)

National Context

K. van Berkel et al. (eds.), *A History of Science in the Netherlands* (Leiden 1999)

W. Frijhoff, *La société Néerlandaise et ses gradués, 1575-1814* (Amsterdam 1981)

W. Frijhoff and M. Spies, *1650. Bevochten eendracht* (The Hague 1999)

J. Israel, *The Dutch Republic. Its Rise, Greatness and Fall, 1477-1806* (Oxford 1995)

G. Jensma and H. de Vries, *Veranderingen in het hoger onderwijs in Nederland tussen 1815 en 1940* (Hilversum 1997)

G.A. Lindeboom, *Geschiedenis van de medische wetenschap in Nederland* (Bussum 1972)

P. de Rooy, *Republiek van rivaliteiten. Nederland sinds 1813* (Amsterdam 2002)

B. Theunissen, *'Nut en nog eens nut'. Wetenschapsbeelden van Nederlandse natuuronderzoekers, 1800-1900* (Hilversum 2000)

General

Leidse universiteit 400. Stichting en eerste bloei 1575-ca. 1650 Catalogus Rijksmuseum (Amsterdam 1975)

T.H. Lunsingh Scheurleer and G.H.M. Posthumus Meyjes (eds.), *Leiden University in the Seventeenth*

Century. An Exchange of Learning (Leiden 1975)

W. Otterspeer (ed.), *Een Universiteit herleeft. Wetenschapsbeoefening aan de Leidse Universiteit vanaf de tweede helft van de negentiende eeuw* (Leiden 1984)

Pallas Leidensis MCMXXV (Leiden 1925)

H.J. de Jonge and W. Otterspeer (eds.), *Altijd een vonk of twee. De Universiteit Leiden van 1975 tot 2000* (Leiden 2000)

Administration

H.L. Clotz, *Hochschule für Holland. Die Universität Leiden im Spannungsfeld zwischen Provinz, Stadt und Kirche, 1575-1619* (Stuttgart 1998)

J.A. van Dorsten, *Poets, Patrons, and Professors. Sir Philip Sidney, Daniel Rogers and the Leiden Humanists* (Leiden 1962)

C.L. Heesakkers and W. Reinders, *Genoeglijk bovenal zijn mij de Muzen. De neolatijnse dichter Janus Dousa (1545-1604)* (Leiden 1993)

P.C. Molhuysen, *De voorrechten der Leidsche Universiteit* (Amsterdam 1924)

H.J. Witkam, *De financiën van de Leidse universiteit in de zestiende eeuw* (5 vols., Leiden 1979-1982)

S. Groenveld et al. (eds.), *Bestuurders en geleerden* (Leiden 1985)

R.G.H. Sluijter, '*Tot ciraet, vermeerderinge ende heerlijckmaeckinge der uni-* *versiteyt'. Bestuur, instellingen, personeel en financiën van de Leidse universiteit, 1575-1812* (Hilversum 2004)

Motto

P. van Heck, '*Libertatis praesidium. Over de herkomst van een devies*', in *Leids Jaarboekje* 95 (2003) 197-210

H.J. de Jonge, 'Ouderdom en herkomst van het devies der Leidse universiteit', in *Leids Jaarboekje* 70 (1978) 143-146

Anatomy Theatre

J.P. Cavaillé, *Un théatre de la science et de la mort à l'époque baroque: l'amphi-théatre d'anatomie de Leiden* (Fiesola 1990)

T. Huisman, *The Finger of God. Anatomical Practice in 17th Century Leiden* (Leiden 2008)

Library

C. Bergvens-Stevelinck, *Magna Commoditas. Geschiedenis van de Leidse universiteitsbibliotheek 1575-2000* (Leiden 2001)

Botanical Garden

L.G.M. Baas Becking and H. Veendorp, *Hortus Botanicus Lugduno-Batavus 1587-1937* (Haarlem 1938)

W.K.H. Karstens, *De Leidse Hortus, een botanische erfenis* (Zwolle 1982)
L.A. Tjon Sie Fat (ed.), *The Authentic Garden* (Leiden 1991)

Administration of Law
P.A.M. Geurts, *Het eerste grote conflict over de eigen rechtspraak der Leidse universiteit* (Utrecht 1964)
M.F.M. Wingens, 'Zur Vermeidung der Schande: Organisation und straf-rechtliche Tätigkeit der Universitätsgerichte in der Republik der Niederlände (1575-1811)', in H. Mohnhaupt and D. Simon (ed.), *Vorträge zur Justizforschung. Geschichte und Theorie* (Frankfurt am Main 1992) 79-100

Lectures
P.A.M. Geurts, *Voorgeschiedenis van het Statencollege te Leiden 1575-1593* (Leiden 1984)
G.H.M. Posthumus Meyjes, *Geschiedenis van het Waalse college te Leiden, 1606-1699* (Leiden 1975)

University Printers
R. Breugelmans, *Christoffel Plantijn in Leiden (1583-1585)* (Leiden 1989)
P.G. Hoftijzer, *Pieter van der Aa (1659-1733). Leids drukker en boekverkoper* (Hilversum 1999)

O.S. Lankhorst and P.G. Hoftijzer, *Drukkers, boekverkopers en lezers in Nederland tijdens de Republiek* (The Hague 1995)
A. Willems, *Les Elzeviers* (Nieuwkoop 1974)

Engineering School
C.A. Davids, 'Universiteiten, illustere scholen en de verspreiding van technische kennis in Nederland', in *Batavia Academica* 8 (1990) 4-34
P.J. van Winter, *Hoger beroepsonderwijs avant-la-lettre. Bemoeiingen met de vorming van landmeters en ingenieurs bij de Nederlandse universiteiten van de 17e en 18e eeuw* (Amsterdam 1988)

Early Physics Laboratory
P.R. de Clercq, *Het Leids Fysisch Kabinet* (Leiden 1989)
P.R. de Clercq, *At the Sign of the Oriental Lamp. The Musschenbroek workshop in Leiden 1660-1750* (Rotterdam 1997)

Early Chemistry Laboratory
W.P. Jorissen, *Het Chemisch (Thans Anorganisch Chemisch) Laboratorium der Universiteit te Leiden van 1859-1909 en de Chemische Laboratoria dier Universiteit vóór dat tijdvak en zij, die er doceerden* (Leiden 1909)

Herbarium

W.A. Goddijn, ''s Rijks Herbarium 1830-1930', in *Mededeelingen van 's Rijks Herbarium, Leiden* 62b (1931) 1-53

Observatory

G. van Herk, *De Leidse sterrenwacht. Vier eeuwen wacht bij dag en nacht* (Zwolle 1983)

Printroom

Het Leidse Prentenkabinet. De geschiedenis van de verzameling (Baarn 1994)

Museum of Ethnology

R. Effert, *Volkenkundig verzamelen. Het Koninklijk Kabinet van Zeldzaamheden en het Rijks Ethnografisch Museum, 1816-1883* (Leiden 2003)

G. van Wengen, *Wat is er te doen in Volkenkunde? De bewogen geschiedenis van het Rijksmuseum voor Volkenkunde in Leiden* (Leiden 2002)

Museum of Natural History

Gijzen, *'s Rijks Museum van Natuurlijke Historie 1820-1915* (Rotterdam 1938)

L.B. Holthuis, *Rijksmuseum van Natuurlijke Historie 1820-1958* (Leiden 1958)

'Rijksmuseum van Geologie en Mineralogie 1878-1978', in *Scripta Geologica* 48 (1978) 3-96

Museum of Antiquities

R.B. Halbertsma, *Scholars, Travellers, and Trade. The Pioneer Years of the National Museum of Antiquities, 1818-1840* (London 2003)

H.D. Schneider, *Rijksmuseum van Oudheden* (Haarlem 1981)

FACULTIES

Theology

W.J. van Asselt, *Amicitia Dei: een onderzoek naar de structuur van de theologie van Johannes Coccejus (1603-1669)* (Utrecht 1988)

W.J. van Asselt et al. (eds.), *Een richtingenstrijd in de Gereformeerde Kerk. Voetianen en coccejanen 1650-1750* (Zoetermeer 1994)

P. Bange et al. (eds.), *Kerk en Verlichting* (Zwolle 1990)

C. Bangs, *Arminius. A Study in the Dutch Reformation* (New York 1981)

J. van den Berg, 'Orthodoxy, Rationalism and the World in Eighteenth-century Holland', in D. Baker (ed.), *Sanctity and Secularity: the Church and the World* (Oxford 1973) 173-192

J. van den Berg, *Een Leids pleidooi voor*

verdraagzaamheid. *Het optreden van
Jan Jacob Schultens in de zaak-Van der
Os* (Leiden 1976)

L.J.M. Bosch, *Petrus Bertius 1565-1629*
(Nijmegen 1979)

A. Eekhof, *De theologische faculteit te
Leiden in de zeventiende eeuw*
(Utrecht 1921)

O. Fatio, *Méthode et théologie. Lambert
Daneau et les débuts de la scolastique
réformée* (Geneva 1976)

J. van Genderen, *Herman Witsius. Bijdrage
tot de kennis der gereformeerde
theologie* (The Hague 1953)

H. Honders, *Andreas Rivetus als
invloedrijk gereformeerd theoloog in
Holland's bleoitijd* (The Hague 1930)

C. de Jong, *De irenische ecclesiologie van
Franciscus Junius (1545-1602)*
(Nieuwkoop 1980)

H.J. de Jonge, *De bestudering van het
Nieuwe Testament aan de
Noordnederlandse universiteiten en
het Remonstrants Seminarie van 1575
tot 1700* (Amsterdam 1980)

A.J. Lamping, *Johannes Polyander. Een
dienaar van Kerk en Universiteit*
(Leiden 1980)

W. Nijenhuis, *Adrianus Saravia (c. 1532-
1613)* (Leiden 1980)

H.W.M. van de Sandt, *Joan Alberti, een
Nederlands theoloog en classicus in de
achttiende eeuw* (Utrecht 1984)

L. Rimbault, *Piere du Moulin 1568-1658.
Un pasteur classique à l'âge classique*
(Paris 1966)

C. Sepp, *Het godgeleerd onderwijs in
Nederland gedurende de 16e en 17e
eeuw* (2 vols., Leiden 1873, 1874)

P.L. Slis, *L.W.E. Rauwenhoff (1828-1889).
Apologeet van het modernisme*
(Kampen 2003)

Law

M. Ahsmann, *Collegia en colleges.
Juridisch onderwijs aan de Leidse
universiteit 1575-1630* (Groningen 1990)

G.C.J.J. van den Bergh, *The Life and Work
of Gerard Noodt (1647-1725). Dutch
Legal Scholarship between Humanism
and Enlightenment* (Oxford 1988)

G.C.J.J. van den Bergh, *Die Holländische
elegante Schule* (Frankfurt am Main
2002)

Jan Drentje, *Thorbecke. Een filosoof in de
politiek* (Amsterdam 2004)

R. Feenstra, *Legal Scholarship and
Doctrines of Private Law, 13th-18th
Centuries* (Leiden 1996)

R. Feenstra and C.D.J. Waal, *Seventeenth-
Century Leiden Law Professors and
Their Influence on the Development of
the Civil Law. A Study of Bronchorst,
Vinnius and Voet* (Amsterdam 1975)

C.J.H. Jansen, *Natuurrecht of Romeins
recht. Een studie over leven en werk van
F.A. van der Marck (1719-1800) in het
licht van de opvattingen van zijn tijd*
(Leiden 1987)

C.J.H. Jansen, *Van Kemper tot Hamaker.
Een onderzoek naar de encyclopedie*

van het recht in de negentiende eeuw
(Zwolle 1990)

E. Poortinga, *De scheiding tussen publiek-
en privaatrecht bij Johan Rudolph
Thorbecke (1798-1872)* (Nijmegen
1987)

I.H. Stamhuis, *'Cijfers en Aequaties' en
'Kennis der Staatskrachten'. Statistiek
in Nederland in de negentiende eeuw*
(Amsterdam 1989)

T.J. Veen and P.C. Knop (eds.), *Zestig
juristen. Bijdragen tot een beeld van de
geschiedenis der Nederlandse
rechtswetenschap* (Zwolle 1987)

Medicine

J.A.J. Barge, *Het geneeskundig onderwijs
aan de Leidse universiteit in de 18e eeuw*
(Leiden 1934)

E.D. Baumann, *Fraençois dele Boe Sylvius*
(Leiden 1949)

A.L. Bierman, *Van artsenijmengkunde
naar artsenijbereidkunde.
Ontwikkelingen in de Nederlandse
farmacie in de negentiende eeuw*
(Amsterdam 1988)

H. Beukers and J. Moll (eds.), *Clinical
Teaching, Past and Present*
(Amsterdam 1989)

A.M. Elshout, *Het Leids cabinet der
anatomie uit de 18e eeuw. De betekenis
van een wetenschappelijke collectie als
cultuurhistorisch monument* (Leiden
1952)

R. Knoeff, *Herman Boerhaave (1668-1738).
Calvinist Chemist and Physician*
(Cambridge 2000)

J.E. Kroon, *Bijdragen tot de geschiedenis
van het geneeskundig onderwijs aan
de Leidsche universiteit 1575-1625*
(Leiden 1911)

M.M. Lamens-van Malenstein, *Oefening
en bespiegeling. Het verloskundig
onderwijs van M.S. du Pui (1754-1834)
te Leiden* (Rotterdam 1997)

G.A. Lindeboom, *Herman Boerhaave.
The Man and His Work* (London 1968)

G.A. Lindeboom, *Florentius Schuyl
(1619-1669) en zijn betekenis voor het
Cartesianisme in de geneeskunde*
(The Hague 1974)

H. Punt, *Bernard Siegfried Albinus
(1697-1770). On 'Human Nature'.
Anatomical and Physiological Ideas
in Eighteenth-Century Leiden*
(Amsterdam 1983)

L.J. Rather, *Mind and Body in Eighteenth-
Century Medicine. A Study Based on
Jerome Gaub's De regimine mentis*
(London 1965)

J. Schouten, *Johannes Walaeus. Zijn
betekenis voor de verbreiding van de
leer van de bloedsomloop* (Assen 1972)

M.J. Sirks (ed.), *Botany in the Netherlands*
(Leiden 1935)

W.T. Stearn, *The influence of Leyden on
Botany in the Seventeenth and
Eighteenth Century* (Leiden 1961)

G. van der Waa, *De irritabilitate. Een
onderzoek naar de betekenis van het
irritabiliteitsbegrip in de geschiedenis*

van de achttiende-eeuwse fysiologie (Rotterdam 1992)

P. van der Zwaag, *Wouter van Doeveren (1730-1783)* (Assen 1970)

Philosophy and Natural Sciences

E.P. Bos and H.A. Krop (ed.), *Franco Burgersdijk (1590-1635). Neo-Aeristotelianism in Leiden* (Amsterdam 1993)

D. van Delft, *Freezing Physics: Heike Kamerlingh Onnes and the Quest for Cold* (Amsterdam 2008)

P. Dibon, *L'Enseigement Philosophique dans les Universités Néerlandaises à l'Époque Pré-Cartésienne (1575-1650)* (Leiden 1954)

S.W. Hamers-van Duynen, *Hieronymus David Gaubius (1705-1780). Zijn correspondentie met Antonio Nunes Ribeiro Sanches en andere tijdgenoten* (Amsterdam 1978)

J.E. Hofmann, *Frans van Schooten der Jüngere* (Wiesbaden 1962)

J.A. van Maanen, *Facets of Seventeenth Century Mathematics in the Netherlands* (Utrecht 1987)

C. de Pater, *Petrus van Musschenbroek (1692-1761), een newtoniaans natuuronderzoeker* (Leiden 1979)

C. de Pater (ed.), *Willem Jacob 's Gravesande. Welzijn, wijsbegeerte en wetenschap* (Baarn 1988)

E.G. Ruestow, *Physics at 17th and 18th-Century Leiden* (The Hague 1973)

G.A. Steffens, *Pieter Nieuwland en het evenwicht* (Zwolle 1964)

C.L. Thijssen-Schoute, *Nederlands Cartesianisme* (Amsterdam 1954)

T. Verbeek, *Descartes and the Dutch. Early Reactions to Cartesian Philosophy, 1637-1650* (Carbondale 1992)

R. Vermij, *Secularisering en natuurwetenschap in de zeventiende en achttiende eeuw: Bernard Nieuwentijt* (Amsterdam 1991)

H. Wansink, *Politieke wetenschappen aan de Leidse Universiteit, 1575-ca. 1650* (Utrecht 1981)

G. Wiesenfeldt, *Leerer Raum in Minervas Haus. Experimentelle Naturlehre an der Universität Leiden, 1675-1715* (Amsterdam 2002)

Humanities

B. Becker-Cantarino, *Daniel Heinsius* (Boston 1978)

S. Bugter, *J.F. Gronovius en de Annales van Tacitus* (Leiden 1980)

P. Dibon and F. Waquet, *Johannes Fredericus Gronovius. Pèlerin de la République des Lettres* (Geneva 1984)

K.A. Enenkel and C. Heesakkers (ed.), *Lipsius in Leiden. Studies in the Life and Works of a Great Humanist* (Voorthuizen 1997)

A. Gerlo (ed.), *Juste Lipse (1547-1606)* (Brussels 1988)

J.G. Gerretzen, *Schola Hemsterhusiana. De herleving der Grieksche studiën aan de*

Nederlandsche universiteiten in de achttiende eeuw van Perizonius tot en met Valckenaer (Nijmegen 1940)

A. Grafton, *Joseph Scaliger. A Study in the History of Classical Scholarship* (2 vols., Oxford, 1983, 1993)

E. Hulshoff Pol, *Studia Ruhnkeniana. Enige hoofdstukken over het leven en werk van David Ruhnkenius (1723-1798)* (Leiden 1953)

G. Karstens, *100 jaar Nederlandse philologie. M. de Vries en zijn school* (Leiden 1949)

A. van der Lem, *Johan Huizinga. Leven en werk in beelden en documenten* (Amsterdam 1993)

P. Leroy, *Le dernier voyage à Paris et en Bourgogne, 1640-1643, du réformé Claude Saumaise* (Amsterdam 1983)

L.H. Maas, *Pro Patria. Werken, leven en streven van de literatuurhistoricus Gerrit Kalff (1856-1923)* (Hilversum 1998)

T.J. Meijer, *kritiek als herwaardering. Het levenswerk van Jacob Perizonius (1651-1715)* (Leiden 1971)

M. Morford, *Stoics and Neostoics. Rubens and the Circle of Lipsius* (Princeton 1991)

J. Noordegraaf, *Norm, geest en geschiedenis. Nederlandse taalkunde in de negentiende eeuw* (Leiden 1985)

C.S.M. Rademaker, *Leven en werk van Gerardus Joannes Vossius (1577-1649)* (Hilversum 1999)

D.C.A.J. Schouten, *Het Grieks aan de Nederlandse universiteiten in de negentiende eeuw* (Utrecht 1964)

J. Tollebeek, *De toga van Fruin. Denken overgeschiedenis in Nederland sinds 1860* (Amsterdam 1990)

Oriental Studies

J. Brugman and F. Schröder, *Arabic Studies in the Netherlands* (Leiden 1979)

W.M.C. Juynboll, *Zeventiende-eeuwsche beoefenaars van het Arabisch in Nederland* (Utrecht 1931)

J. Nat, *Studie van de oostersche talen in de 18e en 19e eeuw* (Purmerend 1929)

W. Otterspeer (ed.), *Leiden Oriental Connections 1850-1940* (Leiden 1989)

P.T. van Rooden, *Constantijn l'Empereur (1591-1648). Professor Hebreeuws te Leiden* (Leiden 1985)

J.P. Vogel, *The Contribution of the University of Leiden to Oriental Research* (Leiden 1954)

W.D. van Wijngaarden, *Van Heurnius tot Boeser. Drie eeuwen Egyptologie in Nederland (1620-1935)*. (Leiden 1935)

Public Image

J. Bientjes, *Holland und der Holländer im Urteil deutscher Reisender 1400-1800* (Groningen 1967)

R. Feenstra and C. Coppens (eds.), *Die rechtswissenschaftlichen Beziehungen zwischen den Niederlanden und*

Deutschland in historischer Sicht
(Nijmegen 1991)

S.A. Knöll, *Creating Academic
Communities. Funeral monuments to
professors at Oxford, Leiden and
Tübingen, 1580-1700* (Oss 2003)

H. de Ridder-Symoens and J.M. Fletcher
(ed.), *Academic Relations between the
Low Countries and the British Isles
1450-1700* (Gent 1989)

E. Hulshoff Pol, 'What about the library?
Travellers' comments on the Leiden
Library in the 17th and 18th century', in
Quaerendo 5 (1975) 166-179

J.N. Jacobsen Jensen, *Reizigers te
Amsterdam* (Amsterdam 1919)

C.S. Maffioli and L.C. Palm (eds.), *Italian
Scientists in the Low Countries in 17th
and 18th Centuries* (Amsterdam 1989)

H. Schneppen, *Niederländische
Universitäten und Deutsches
Geistesleben. Von der Gründung der
Universität Leiden bis ins späte 18.*

Jahrhundert (Münster 1960)

C.D. van Strien, *Touring the Low
Countries: accounts of the British
travellers, 1660-1720* (Amsterdam 1998)

Second World War

P.J. Idenburg, *De Leidse universiteit
1928-1946. Vernieuwing en verzet*
(The Hague 1978)

Student Life

*Gedenkboek van het Leidsche
Studentencorps* (Leiden 1919)

*Geschiedboek van de Leidse Studenten
Vereniging Minerva, 1814-1989*
(Leiden 1989)

*Geschiedenis van het Leidsche Studenten
Corps* (Leiden 1950)

A.C.J. de Vrankrijker, *Vier Eeuwen
Nederlandsch Studentenleven*
(Voorburg 1939)

Acknowledgments

Anyone who sets out to write a history of a university needs a great deal of help. I should like to express my thanks to the deans of the major faculties who supplied me with information; I was compelled to consult Frans Saris, Carel Stolker and Eduard Klasen on more than one occasion. The book also benefited from the knowledge and experience of Henk Jan de Jonge and Pieter Janse. Thanks are due to my PhD student Martine Zoeteman, who provided a significant proportion of the statistics, and to Yvo van Marle, who found other statistics and collated them as one whole. I also wish to express my gratitude to John Kroes and Corrie van Maris for their wise counsel, Arlette van Kouwenhoven and Kasper van Ommen for collecting the illustrations, Jos van den Broek for allowing me to use his photographs, and Pieter Slaman for his indefatigable support. I should also like to thank the staff of Amsterdam University Press for the enthusiasm and discernment with which they have approached this project, and Beverley Jackson for translating the book into English in the spirit of creative collaboration. Whatever shortcomings the book may have are of course entirely my own responsibility.

Index

O

Offredi, C. 64
Oldenbarneveldt, J. van 52
Oomen, C.P.C.M. 211-212, 222
Oort, J.H. 159-160
Oosterhoff, L.J. 160
Oppenheim, J. 155, 159
Orlers, J.J. 22-23, 105
Os, D.P. den 262
Oven, J.C. van 160

P

Palm, J.H. van der 152
Paul 29, 67
Pauw, A. 33
Peerlkamp, P. Hofman 119
Peursen, C.A. van 160
Philip van Marnix 116
Plantijn, P. 98
Plato 28
Pliny 51
Poellnitz, von 88
Polyander, J. 48, 67
Ponec, V. 160
Powell, P. 87
Pynacker, C. 47

Q

Querido, A. 160
Quispel, A. 160

R

Rademaker, G.G.J. 160
Radzivill, J. 85, 92
Raei, J. de 58-59
Ramus 15

Raphelengius, F. 52
Rauwenhoff, L.W.E. 155
Ray, J. 63
Reinwardt, C.G.C. 151
Reuvens, C.J.C. 152
Reve, K. van het 284
Revius, J. 67
Rijk, L.M. de 160
Rivet, A. 44
Romein, J. 284
Rood, J.J. van 160
Rosenstein, S.S. 155
Rüegg, W. 9
Rypperda Wierdsma, J.V. 160

S

Salmasius, C. 44-45, 67
Saravia, A. 52
Scaliger, J.J. 36, 44-45
Schaap, J.W. 135
Schnitzler, A. 180
Scholten, J.H. 155
Schrant, J.M. 155
Schreinemakers, F.A.H. 155
Schulte Northolt, J.W. 160
Scriverius, P. 106
Seneca 29
Senguerd, W. 60
Seyss-Inquart, A. 122
Shils, E. 278
Snellius, R. 89
Snouck Hurgronje, C. 159, 185, 239
Snow, C.P. 155
Sobels, F.H. 160
Sopper, A.J. de 147
Sosius, T. 52

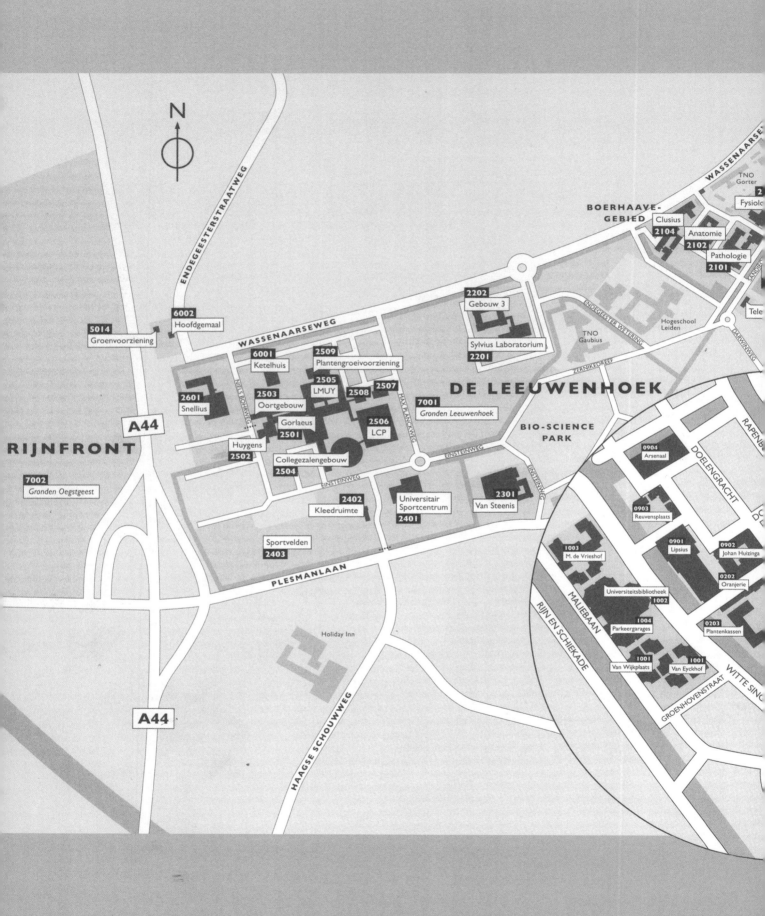